Tea & Savories

Tea & Savories

Delightful Teatime Treats

hm | books

books

EDITOR *Lorna Reeves*
CREATIVE DIRECTOR/PHOTOGRAPHY *Mac Jamieson*
ART DIRECTOR *Cailyn Haynes*
ASSOCIATE EDITOR *Betty Terry*
COPY EDITOR *Nancy Ogburn*
EDITORIAL ASSISTANT *Melissa L. Brinley*
STYLIST *Lucy W. Herndon*
SENIOR PHOTOGRAPHERS *John O'Hagan,
Marcy Black Simpson*
PHOTOGRAPHERS *Jim Bathie,
William Dickey, Stephanie Welbourne*
TEST KITCHEN PROFESSIONAL *Janet Lambert*
CONTRIBUTING TEST KITCHEN PROFESSIONALS
Virginia Hornbuckle, Loren Wood
SENIOR DIGITAL IMAGING SPECIALIST *Delisa McDaniel*
DIGITAL IMAGING SPECIALIST *Clark Densmore*

hm
hoffmanmedia

CHAIRMAN OF THE BOARD/CEO
Phyllis Hoffman DePiano
PRESIDENT/COO *Eric W. Hoffman*
PRESIDENT/CCO *Brian Hart Hoffman*
EVP/CFO *Mary P. Cummings*
EVP/OPERATIONS & MANUFACTURING
Greg Baugh
VP/DIGITAL MEDIA *Jon Adamson*
VP/EDITORIAL *Cindy Smith Cooper*
VP/ADMINISTRATION *Lynn Lee Terry*

First published in 2015 by Hoffman Media, LLC
1900 International Park Drive, Suite 50
Birmingham, Alabama 35243
hoffmanmedia.com

ISBN 978-1-940772-15-8
Printed in Mexico

ON THE COVER: Roasted Vegetable–Cream Cheese Tea
Sandwiches (page 103), Cucumber Canapés (page 83),
Apricot-Chive Chicken Salad in Puff Pastry Shells (page 58)
Recipe development and food styling by Janet Lambert
Photography by Jim Bathie | Photo styling by Lucy W. Herndon

GREEN GRAPE AND KIWI
CHICKEN SALAD SANDWICHES
(recipe on page 98)

Contents

Introduction

DAINTY TEA SANDWICHES filled with thinly sliced cucumber, creamy chicken salad, or flavorful smoked salmon are the foods afternoon-tea aficionados have come to expect on the savories level of a traditional three-tiered stand. Often served as the second course in the United States after warm scones with accompaniments of clotted cream, lemon curd, and jam have been happily eaten, the savories usually take first billing in Britain. The order in which these first two courses are presented is widely and politely disputed—with eloquent reasoning on both sides of the debate—but for most lovers of afternoon tea, the important thing is that both courses be served so they can be properly and leisurely enjoyed.

A creative host might wish to expand the offerings beyond simple tea sandwiches to include fanciful canapés and savory tartlets. And if the occasion takes place closer to lunchtime, then a heartier menu of soups, salads, and quiches might be desirable, either en lieu of or alongside the tiered stand.

This collection of recipes, some of which are gluten-free, offers an array of flavorful and pretty options that will satisfy even the most discriminating diner. Most were created in *TeaTime*'s test kitchen exclusively for this book, while others were contributed by select tearooms or have previously graced the pages of the magazine. Whatever the source, these soups and salads, quiches and tartlets, and tea sandwiches and canapés will be well received at any occasion afternoon tea is served, especially when accompanied with the right infusion. Our pairing guidelines (page 11) and tea-steeping basics (page 10) will be extremely helpful in choosing and preparing the perfect pot of tea for your guests to savor at their next teatime.

CURRIED CHICKEN SALAD
(recipe on page 32)

Tea-Steeping *Guide*

The quality of the tea served at a tea party is as important as the food and the décor. To be sure your infusion is successful every time, here are some basic guidelines to follow.

WATER

Always use the best water possible. If the water tastes good, so will your tea. Heat the water on the stove top or in an electric kettle to the desired temperature. A microwave oven is not recommended.

TEMPERATURE

Heating the water to the correct temperature is arguably one of the most important factors in making a great pot of tea. Pouring boiling water on green, white, or oolong tea leaves can result in a very unpleasant brew. Always refer to the tea purveyor's packaging for specific instructions, but in general, use 170° to 195° water for these delicate tea types. Reserve boiling (212°) water for black and puerh teas, as well as herbal and fruit tisanes.

TEAPOT

If the teapot you plan to use is delicate, warm it with hot tap water first to avert possible cracking. Discard this water before adding the tea leaves or tea bags.

TEA

Use the highest-quality tea you can afford, whether loose leaf or prepackaged in bags or sachets. Remember that these better teas can often be steeped more than once. When using loose-leaf tea, generally use 1 generous teaspoon of dry leaf per 8 ounces of water, and use an infuser basket. For a stronger infusion, add another teaspoonful or two of dry tea leaf.

TIME

As soon as the water reaches the correct temperature for the type of tea, pour it over the leaves or tea bag in the teapot, and cover the pot with a lid. Set a timer—usually 1 to 2 minutes for whites and oolongs; 2 to 3 minutes for greens; and 3 to 5 minutes for blacks, puerhs, and herbals. (Steeping tea longer than recommended can yield a bitter infusion.) When the timer goes off, remove the infuser basket or the tea bags from the teapot.

ENJOYMENT

For best flavor, serve the tea as soon as possible. Keep the beverage warm atop a lighted warmer or under your favorite tea cozy if necessary.

Tea-Pairing Guide

CHOOSING A TEA that perfectly complements the menu for afternoon tea is a critical part of hosting a successful event. When selecting infusions to accompany savory morsels, keep in mind that the flavor of the tea should enhance—rather than compete with or overpower—the flavors and mouthfeel of the food, and vice versa. For that reason, we recommend reserving delicate teas, such as the whites, for drinking on their own. Greens, blacks, puerhs, and many oolongs are excellent choices for serving alongside the savory teatime course. The following guide offers recommendations of teas to pair with the various flavor profiles of many recipes in this book, but it should by no means be considered definitive:

CHEESE (MILD) Golden Tips Assam Black Tea, Ceylon Blackwood Estate Black Tea, Nepal Mist Valley Black Tea

CHEESE (STRONG) Formosa Oolong Tea, Golden Monkey Black Tea, Gunpowder Green Tea

EGGS & POULTRY Baked Tie Kuan Yin Oolong Tea, Dragonwell Green Tea, Darjeeling 2nd Flush Black Tea

FRUIT Formosa Jade Oolong Tea, Darjeeling 1st Flush Black Tea, Oriental Beauty Oolong Tea, Vietnamese OP Black Tea

RED MEAT Ceylon UVA Highlands Black Tea, Winey Keemun Black Tea, Russian Caravan Black Tea

SALAD & VEGETABLES Luan Guapian Green Tea, Keemun Spring Mao Feng Black Tea, Japanese Sencha Green Tea

SEAFOOD Gyokuro Green Tea, Tung Ting Oolong Tea, Ceylon Lover's Leap Black Tea, Golden Tips Assam Black Tea

SMOKED MEAT Vietnam Imperial Oolong Tea, Assam Black Tea, Irish Breakfast Black Tea Blend

SPICY Superior Grade Puerh Tea, Ceylon Highlands Black Tea, Tippy Yunnan Black Tea, Assam Doomni Estate Black Tea

A prudent host will prepare the chosen tea in advance of the event to verify that the pairing is pleasing and to determine the most beneficial water temperature and steep time. This will ensure good tea and a delightful teatime. For a list of purveyors of fine teas such as these, turn to page 132.

Soups & Salads

BLACKBERRY-BRIE
CHICKEN SALAD
(recipe on page 35)

Red Quinoa Salad in Frico Cups

Gluten-free | *Yield: 12 servings* | *Preparation: 15 minutes*

2 cups cooked red quinoa
½ cup chopped dates
⅓ cup chopped roasted pistachios
¼ cup finely chopped carrot
2 tablespoons chopped green onion (green parts only)
2 tablespoons chopped cilantro
1 recipe Honey-Sherry Vinaigrette (recipe follows)
1 cup watercress
12 Parmesan Frico Cups (recipe on page 20)
Garnish: carrot curl*

• In a medium bowl, combine quinoa, dates, pistachios, carrot, green onion, and cilantro, stirring to blend. Add enough Honey-Sherry Vinaigrette to moisten salad so that it will hold together when scooped. Stir gently to coat.
• Lay watercress leaves in bottoms of frico cups, and top each with a scoop of quinoa salad.
• Garnish each serving with a carrot curl, if desired.
• Serve immediately with remaining vinaigrette on the side, if desired.

To make carrot curls, draw a vegetable peeler across the side of a peeled carrot.

Honey-Sherry Vinaigrette

Gluten-free | *Yield: ½ cup* | *Preparation: 40 minutes*

¼ cup extra-virgin olive oil
¼ cup sherry vinegar*
1 teaspoon fresh lemon juice
1 teaspoon Dijon-style mustard
1 teaspoon finely chopped shallot
1 tablespoon honey
½ teaspoon salt
¼ teaspoon ground black pepper

• In a small jar with a screw-top lid, combine olive oil, vinegar, lemon juice, mustard, shallot, honey, salt, and pepper. Shake vigorously until emulsified. Let stand at room temperature for 30 minutes to allow flavors to develop.
• Use immediately, or refrigerate until needed. (Let come to room temperature before using, shaking again to blend.)

Use aged sherry vinegar, not sherry cooking wine, which has a higher salt content and a different flavor.

Chilled Cantaloupe Soup

Gluten-free | *Yield: 8 (½-cup) servings*
Preparation: 15 minutes | *Refrigerate: 4 hours*

4 cups cubed cantaloupe
½ cup fresh orange juice
1 tablespoon fresh lime juice
Garnish: fresh basil leaves, prosciutto*

• In the container of a blender, combine cantaloupe, orange juice, and lime juice. Pulse until well blended and smooth.
• Transfer soup mixture to a covered container, and refrigerate until cold, approximately 4 hours.
• Serve cold.
• Garnish individual servings with fresh basil and prosciutto, if desired.

If desired, cut small flower shapes from prosciutto for garnish.

Baby English Pea Salad in Artichoke Cups

Gluten-free | *Yield: 6 servings*
Preparation: 15 minutes | *Refrigerate: 4 hours*

1 cup baby (petite) frozen green peas
1 tablespoon finely minced shallot
1 tablespoon sweet pickle relish
2 teaspoons diced pimiento
2 tablespoons finely diced celery
2 teaspoons mayonnaise
1 teaspoon fresh lemon juice
⅛ teaspoon salt
⅛ teaspoon ground black pepper
6 canned artichoke bottoms
Garnish: frisée

• Place frozen green peas in a colander, and hold under hot running tap water for 30 seconds. Shake colander well, and set aside to drain.
• In a medium bowl, combine shallot, pickle relish, pimiento, and celery. Set aside.
• In a small bowl, combine mayonnaise, lemon juice, salt, and pepper, whisking well.
• Add peas and mayonnaise mixture to shallot mixture, stirring just until combined.
• Cover, and refrigerate until cold, approximately 4 hours.
• Divide salad evenly among artichoke bottoms.
• Garnish with frisée, if desired.

Mushroom-Thyme Soup

Yield: 6 (½-cup) servings | *Preparation: 20 minutes*
Cook: 30 minutes

4 tablespoons salted butter
2 cups coarsely chopped white button mushrooms
1 cup chopped sweet onion
2 teaspoons minced garlic
4 tablespoons all-purpose flour
1 (32-ounce) carton beef stock
1 tablespoon fresh thyme leaves
⅛ teaspoon ground nutmeg
⅛ teaspoon ground black pepper
⅓ cup heavy whipping cream
1 tablespoon dry sherry
Garnish: fresh thyme

• In a large saucepan, melt butter over medium-high heat. Add mushrooms and onion, stirring to coat with butter. Reduce heat to low. Cook, stirring occasionally, until vegetables are tender, approximately 8 minutes.
• Add garlic, and cook for 1 minute. Add flour, stirring to blend, and cook for 1 to 2 minutes. Add stock, thyme, nutmeg, and pepper, and bring to a boil. Reduce heat to a simmer. Cook for 30 minutes.
• Add cream and sherry, stirring to incorporate.
• Serve warm.
• Garnish individual servings with fresh thyme, if desired.

"*I live on good soup,*
not on fine words."

—Molière

Kitchen Tip: *Use preshredded Parmesan cheese to make Parmesan Frico Cups. It bakes into a firmer, sturdier basket.*

Spring Salad in Frico Cups

Gluten-free | *Yield: 8 servings* | *Preparation: 10 minutes*

2 cups spring-mix lettuces
¼ cup radish slices
¼ cup matchstick carrots
2 tablespoons thinly sliced green onion
¼ cup fresh green peas
1 recipe Herbed Champagne Vinaigrette (recipe follows)
8 Parmesan Frico Cups (recipe below)

• Divide lettuces, radish slices, carrots, green onion, and green peas evenly among Parmesan Frico Cups. Drizzle salad with Herbed Champagne Vinaigrette.
• Serve immediately with remaining vinaigrette on the side, if desired.

Herbed Champagne Vinaigrette
Gluten-free | *Yield: ½ cup* | *Preparation: 5 minutes*

¼ cup champagne vinegar
2 teaspoons minced fresh chives
2 teaspoons minced fresh dill
½ teaspoon finely minced shallot
½ teaspoon sugar
¼ teaspoon fine sea salt
⅛ teaspoon ground black pepper
⅓ cup extra-light olive oil

• In a small bowl, combine vinegar, chives, dill, shallot, sugar, salt, and pepper, whisking well. Add olive oil in a slow steady stream, whisking vigorously until emulsified.
• Cover, and let sit at room temperature until ready to use.

Make-Ahead Tip: Best made day of use, but can be refrigerated in a covered container for 2 to 3 days. Let come to room temperature before serving.

Parmesan Frico Cups

Gluten-free | *Yield: varies* | *Preparation: 10 minutes*
Bake: 5 to 8 minutes | *Cool: 15 minutes*

¼ cup shredded Parmesan cheese,
    such as Sargento, per frico cup

• Preheat oven to 350°.
• Line a baking sheet with a silicone baking mat or parchment paper.
• Sprinkle cheese into a 3½- to 4-inch circle on prepared baking sheet. (Make only 8 circles at a time as cheese hardens quickly and becomes difficult to work with.)
• Bake until cheese melts and edges are golden brown, 5 to 8 minutes.

• Using a metal spatula, quickly remove cheese rounds from baking sheet, and drape over an inverted custard cup or the wells of an inverted muffin pan, shaping into ruffled baskets. Let cool completely.
• Remove frico cups from backs of custard cups or muffin pan. Store at room temperature in an airtight container until ready to serve. (Best made day of use.)

Watermelon Gazpacho

Gluten-free | *Yield: 8 (1-cup) servings*
Preparation: 20 minutes | *Refrigerate: 4 hours*

8 cups puréed watermelon (approximately 2 quarts
    cubed or ½ large watermelon)
1 cup coarsely chopped red bell pepper
1 cup coarsely chopped English cucumber
1 cup coarsely chopped red onion
¼ cup fresh cilantro leaves
¼ cup fresh lime juice
Garnish: additional fresh cilantro leaves

• In the work bowl of a food processor, combine watermelon, bell pepper, cucumber, onion, cilantro, and lime juice. Pulse until finely chopped. Transfer mixture to an airtight container, and refrigerate until cold, approximately 4 hours.
• Serve cold.
• Garnish individual servings with a cilantro leaf, if desired.

The Tilted Teacup
Tea Room & Boutique
a servant's heart

In 2011, John Gans was preparing to retire from the U.S. Army after 20 years of service. He had always wanted to start a business, but he didn't know what form it should take. Finally he asked his wife, "What would you want to do?"

"I know this sounds crazy," Aimee replied, "but I've always wanted to open a tearoom." She had no previous restaurant experience, and she even had to explain to her husband what a tearoom is. "Opening a tearoom was always my dream." she explains. "I have a servant's heart—I love to serve people."

The couple took a year to research the idea, and they prayed about it. "We said that if this is God's will for us, He will open doors," Aimee recalls. "And if not, we'll forget it." They found a small, 1904-vintage cottage in Brooksville, Florida, that needed remodeling, and in 2012 they opened The Tilted Teacup.

Two years later, they had already outgrown their tiny space. Local couple Dorothea and Greg Stephens wanted to know if the Stephenses bought the old Roger's Christmas House, which had been a retail destination for tourists from the early 1970s to 2010, would the Ganses consider moving their tearoom there?

Aimee and John jumped at the offer, even though they would, once again, be renovating a house they did not own. The work took seven months and involved rewiring and replumbing the house and refinishing the original hardwood floors. "Our new location opened in November 2014, and the business has grown by leaps and bounds."

Although tea is her passion, Aimee says, "Running a tearoom is the hardest job I've ever had to do." When a customer tells her how much they enjoyed having afternoon tea, it lifts her spirits, she says. "It is completely rewarding."

Lemon-Blueberry Chicken Salad
Gluten-free | *Yield: 5 servings*
Preparation: 30 minutes | *Bake: 25 minutes*

⅔ cup Microwave Lemon Curd (recipe follows)
½ cup vanilla lowfat yogurt
¼ cup mayonnaise
1 teaspoon salt
1 teaspoon lemon extract
2 to 3 cups cubed cooked chicken breast*
¾ cup sliced celery
½ cup sliced green onion
½ cup diced red bell pepper
1½ teaspoons chopped fresh basil
2 cups fresh blueberries
Spring-mix lettuces
Garnish: sliced lemons and fresh basil leaves

• In a bowl, combine Microwave Lemon Curd, yogurt, mayonnaise, salt, and lemon extract, stirring well. Add chicken, celery, green onion, bell pepper, and basil, stirring gently. Add blueberries, folding in gently.
• Cover, and refrigerate for 1 hour to let flavors meld.
• Arrange 1-cup portions on a bed of spring mix.
• Garnish each serving with a lemon slice and a basil leaf, if desired.

Aimee Gans at The Tilted Teacup soaks the chicken in a brine before cooking it, using the following method. In a large bowl, combine 4 cups water, 3 tablespoons salt, and 2 tablespoons sugar, stirring well. Add raw chicken. Cover bowl, and refrigerate for 1 hour. Pat chicken dry, and drizzle with olive oil. Roast in a 350° oven for 25 to 30 minutes.

Microwave Lemon Curd

Gluten-free | *Yield: approximately 1 cup* | *Preparation: 10 minutes*
Microwave: 6 minutes | *Cool: 30 minutes* | *Refrigerate: 4 hours*

3 large eggs
1 cup sugar
½ cup salted butter, melted
½ cup lemon juice
1½ teaspoons fresh lemon zest

• In a glass mixing bowl, beat eggs at high speed with
a mixer until frothy, approximately 1 minute. Add sugar,
melted butter, lemon juice, and lemon zest, beating
at low speed for 30 seconds.
• Microwave on High for 3 minutes. Beat mixture
at low speed for 30 seconds until smooth.
• Microwave on High for 3 minutes more.
Beat mixture again until smooth.
• Transfer lemon curd to another bowl, and let
cool to room temperature. Cover, and refrigerate
until cool and set, approximately 4 hours.
Refrigerate for up to 2 weeks.

Tomato Gazpacho

Gluten-free | *Yield: 8 (1-cup) servings*
Preparation: 15 minutes | *Refrigerate: 6 hours*

5 large ripe tomatoes, peeled and seeded
1 cup coarsely chopped sweet onion
1 cup coarsely chopped English cucumber
½ cup coarsely chopped red bell pepper
½ cup coarsely chopped green bell pepper
½ cup loosely packed parsley leaves
½ cup loosely packed basil leaves
¼ cup canned red pimiento strips
3 tablespoons chopped chives
2 cups beef broth
2 tablespoons fresh lime juice
2 tablespoons fresh lemon juice
1 tablespoon olive oil
1 tablespoon salt
½ teaspoon ground black pepper
Garnish: toasted bread croutons*

• In the work bowl of a food processor or the container of a blender, combine tomatoes, onion, cucumber, bell peppers, parsley, basil, pimiento, chives, broth, lime juice, lemon juice, olive oil, salt, and pepper, pulsing until smooth. (Process in batches, if necessary.)
• Transfer mixture to an airtight container, and refrigerate for 6 hours.
• Serve cold.
• Garnish individual servings with a crouton, if desired.

Using a small, decorative cutter, cut shapes from bread slices. In a nonstick skillet over medium heat, toast bread shapes on both sides. To make gluten-free, use gluten-free bread.

Mini Chicken Taco Salads

Gluten-free | *Yield: 24 salads*
Preparation: 30 minutes | *Bake: 15 to 22 minutes*

24 corn tortillas
3 tablespoons vegetable oil
1 (6-ounce) boneless, skinless chicken breast half
1 tablespoon olive oil
1 teaspoon taco seasoning
¼ teaspoon salt
1 cup finely shredded lettuce
½ cup cooked black beans
¼ cup finely diced red bell pepper
¼ cup finely diced purple onion
1 recipe Creamy Honey-Chipotle Dressing
    (recipe follows)
Garnish: cilantro leaves

• Preheat oven to 350°.
• Spray 2 (12-well) muffin pans with cooking spray. Set aside.
• Using a 3½-inch cutter, cut 24 circles from corn tortillas, discarding scraps.
• Working in small batches, wrap tortilla circles in damp paper towels, and place in a microwave oven. Microwave for a few seconds on High (100 percent power) to soften tortilla circles. Press lightly into prepared wells of muffin pans to form a ruffled cup shape. Lightly brush surface of each tortilla cup with vegetable oil.
• Bake until edges are light golden brown, 5 to 7 minutes.
• Remove tortilla cups from muffin pans, and let cool on wire racks. Store in airtight containers until ready to use. (Best made day of use.)
• Brush chicken breast with olive oil, and then sprinkle both sides with taco seasoning and salt.
• Roast in oven until meat is white and opaque with no pink and juices run clear (170° on a meat thermometer), 10 to 15 minutes.
• Let cool, then chop into ¼-inch pieces. Set aside.
• Fill each shell with lettuce, and top with black beans, bell pepper, onion, and chicken. Drizzle with Creamy Honey-Chipotle Dressing.
• Garnish with cilantro leaves, if desired.
• Serve immediately.

Creamy Honey-Chipotle Dressing

Gluten-free | *Yield: 1 cup* | *Preparation: 5 minutes*

1 cup mayonnaise
2 tablespoons honey
1 lime, juiced
¾ teaspoon ground chipotle pepper
¼ teaspoon salt

• In a small bowl, combine mayonnaise, honey, lime juice, chipotle pepper, and salt, whisking until well blended.
• Cover, and refrigerate for up to 2 days until ready to serve.

*"Variety's the very spice of life,
That gives it all its flavor."*

—William Cowper

Watermelon-Feta Salad

Gluten-free | *Yield: 6 servings* | *Preparation: 15 minutes*

1 (4½-pound) watermelon
1 (8-ounce) block feta cheese
1 teaspoon ground pink peppercorns
1 recipe White Balsamic Vinaigrette (recipe follows)
Garnish: 6 fresh basil leaves, 6 fresh blueberries

• Cut watermelon into 12 (½-inch) slices. Using a 3-inch flower-shaped cutter, cut a flower shape from each watermelon slice. Set aside.
• Cut feta into 6 (¼-inch) slices. Using a 3-inch flower-shaped cutter, cut a flower shape from each feta slice.
• Press ground peppercorns decoratively into sides of each feta flower.
• Stack a watermelon flower, a feta flower, and another watermelon flower on top of each other. Cover, and refrigerate for up to a day until needed.
• Drizzle each stack with White Balsamic Vinaigrette.
• Garnish each stack with a basil leaf and a blueberry, if desired.
• Serve immediately with remaining vinaigrette on the side, if desired.

White Balsamic Vinaigrette

Gluten-free | *Yield: 1 cup* | *Preparation: 5 minutes*

¼ cup white balsamic vinegar
2 tablespoons minced red onion
2 tablespoons minced fresh basil
⅛ teaspoon salt
¾ cup extra-light olive oil

• In a small bowl, combine vinegar, onion, basil, and salt, whisking well. Add olive oil in a slow steady stream, whisking until emulsified. Cover, and refrigerate for up to 2 days until needed.

Creamy Cauliflower-Leek Soup

Gluten-free | *Yield: 10 (½-cup) servings*
Preparation: 20 minutes | *Cook: 20 minutes*

4 tablespoons salted butter
2 cups sliced leeks (white parts only)
1 large head cauliflower, chopped
1 (32-ounce) carton low-sodium chicken stock
½ teaspoon salt
½ cup heavy whipping cream
Garnish: 1 recipe Parmesan Wafers (recipe follows)

• In a large saucepan, melt butter over medium-high heat. Add leeks, and reduce heat to low. Cook until soft, approximately 10 minutes, stirring occasionally.
• Add cauliflower, stock, and salt, and bring to a boil. Reduce heat to simmer. Cook until cauliflower is extremely tender. Remove from heat.
• Using a hand-held immersion blender, purée soup mixture until very smooth. Add cream, stirring to combine.
• Return soup to heat, and let simmer until heated through. Serve warm.
• Garnish individual servings with a Parmesan Wafer, if desired.

Parmesan Wafers

Gluten-free | *Yield: 10 wafers* | *Preparation: 5 minutes*
Bake: 5 to 7 minutes | *Cool: 30 minutes*

⅔ cup grated Parmesan cheese

• Preheat oven to 350°.
• Line a rimmed baking sheet with parchment paper.
• Spread 2 tablespoons cheese into a 1½-inch circle on prepared baking sheet. Repeat 9 times.
• Bake until edges of wafers are golden brown, 5 to 7 minutes. Let cool completely on pan.
• Store wafers in an airtight container. Use the same day.

The Royal Tea Room
& Gift Shoppe
where your heart is

"Sometimes life throws you a curve," says Denise Winter, recalling how she came to open The Royal Tea Room in Tampa, Florida, in 1996. Denise was the general manager of a corporate travel agency when the company was sold, and she found herself without a job. "Opening a tearoom was the next thing in front of me."

The tearoom that was a haven for Denise has become a haven for tea lovers as well. When guests walk through the whimsically decorated gift shop to the tearoom, their cares fall away, and they immediately feel a sense of peace. The elegant European ambiance of The Royal Tea Room lets them know they are in for a pampering experience.

Denise, who has been head chef since day one, takes great pride in the food she serves. She makes everything fresh, the moment customers walk in. But as to afternoon tea, Denise is something of a purist. The Royal Tea Room does not serve lunch. Teas—either a cream tea, a sweets tea, an afternoon tea, or a royal tea—are the only meals offered, and hot tea is the only beverage. "Our guests come for traditional afternoon tea," she explains, and that's what she gives them.

"We know our teas, and we know what we're serving. So we pair our teas with each day's menu," Denise says. And all teas served, branded under the tearoom's own Royal Tea label, are available in the gift shop.

"I do enjoy running a tearoom," Denise explains. "But it's a hard business, so that's where your heart has to be." The pleasure, she says, is "putting smiles on people's faces and having them leave feeling like their souls have been rested, and they have thoroughly enjoyed their time here—you can't ask for more than that."

Cranberry-Chicken Salad
Gluten-free | *Yield: 16 servings*
Preparation: 15 minutes
Refrigerate: 3 to 4 hours

4 cups chopped cooked chicken
¾ cup sour cream
¾ cup dried cranberries
½ cup mayonnaise
1½ tablespoons finely chopped
   green onion
½ teaspoon coarse salt
16 canned artichoke bottoms
Garnish: chopped dried cranberries

• In a large bowl, combine chicken, sour cream, dried cranberries, mayonnaise, green onion, and salt, stirring until thoroughly blended. (If mixture seems dry, add more sour cream, 1 tablespoon at a time.)
• Cover, and refrigerate for 3 to 4 hours to let flavors meld.
• Using a ¼-cup scoop, divide chicken salad among artichoke bottoms.
• Garnish with chopped dried cranberries, if desired.

- Using a hand-held immersion blender, purée soup mixture until very smooth. Return soup to heat, and simmer gently until heated through.
- Serve warm.
- Garnish individual servings with sour cream, if desired.

Grind whole star anise by using a mortar and pestle or an electric spice grinder.

Make-Ahead Tip: *Refrigerate in a covered container for up to a day. Reheat in a saucepan over very low heat.*

Petite Potato Salad Flowers
Gluten-free | *Yield: 12 servings*
Preparation: 35 minutes | *Bake: 20 minutes*
Cool: 1 hour

6 baby variety potatoes, such as baby Yukon golds
1 teaspoon olive oil
⅛ teaspoon salt
⅛ teaspoon ground black pepper
1 large hard-boiled egg, peeled
¼ cup mayonnaise
1 cup sweet gherkin pickles

- Preheat oven to 400°.
- Line a rimmed baking pan with foil.
- In a medium bowl, toss potatoes with olive oil, salt, and pepper. Spread potatoes on prepared pan, and roast until tender when pierced with the tip of a knife, approximately 20 minutes. Let cool completely.
- Push egg through a fine-mesh sieve.
- In a small bowl, combine mayonnaise and egg, reserving some egg for garnish. Set aside.
- Using a sharp paring knife, cut 60 very thin (approximately ⅛-inch-thick) slices from pickles, discarding ends. Set aside.
- Cut each potato in half horizontally. Trim ends of each potato half to level base. Using a melon baller, scoop potato halves, discarding center pulp, to create a cavity. Spoon ½ teaspoon mayonnaise mixture into each cavity.
- Arrange 5 pickle slices in each cavity, overlapping slightly to resemble petals of a flower.
- Garnish center of pickle flowers with a sprinkle of reserved egg.

Make-Ahead Tip: *Potatoes can be roasted a day in advance and refrigerated in a covered container. Mayonnaise mixture can be made a day in advance, and refrigerated in a covered container. Pickles can be sliced a day in advance and refrigerated in a covered container with some pickle juice (drain before using). Assemble up to an hour in advance, and refrigerate, covered, until serving time.*

Ginger-Carrot Soup
Gluten-free | *Yield: 8 (½-cup) servings*
Preparation: 20 minutes | *Cook: 45 minutes*

2 tablespoons salted butter
1 cup chopped sweet onion
4 cups sliced carrots
1 cup low-sodium chicken stock
1½ teaspoons finely grated fresh ginger root
½ teaspoon ground star anise*
½ teaspoon ground turmeric
Garnish: sour cream

- In a large saucepan, melt butter over medium-high heat. Add onion, and reduce heat to low. Cook, stirring constantly, until onion is caramelized and tender, approximately 10 minutes.
- Add carrots, stock, ginger, anise, and turmeric. Bring to a boil, then reduce heat to a simmer. Cook until carrots are very tender, approximately 30 minutes. Remove soup from heat.

Curried Chicken Salad

Gluten-free | *Yield: 8 (½-cup) servings*
Preparation: 15 minutes | *Refrigerate: 4 hours*

½ cup mayonnaise
1 tablespoon fresh lime juice
1 teaspoon honey
½ teaspoon curry powder
½ teaspoon salt
¼ teaspoon ground black pepper
3 cups diced poached chicken
½ cup diced red grapes
½ cup diced yellow apple
⅓ cup diced celery
⅓ cup chopped roasted, salted cashews
Garnish: Bibb lettuce

• In a small bowl, combine mayonnaise, lime juice, honey, curry powder, salt, and pepper, whisking well. Set aside.
• In a large bowl, combine chicken, grapes, apple, and celery, stirring well. Add mayonnaise mixture, stirring to combine.
• Cover, and refrigerate until cold, at least 4 hours. Add cashews, stirring well.
• Garnish individual servings with Bibb lettuce leaves, if desired.
• Serve immediately.

Make-Ahead Tip: *Refrigerate in a covered container for up to 2 days. Add cashews just before serving*

Salmon-Filled Cucumbers

Gluten-free | *Yield: 10 servings*
Preparation: 35 minutes

1 (12-inch) English cucumber
⅔ cup sour cream
2 teaspoons fresh lemon zest
¼ teaspoon salt
1 (4-ounce) package thinly sliced smoked salmon, such as Echo Falls
2 tablespoons caviar, such as black lumpfish
Garnish: fresh dill sprigs

• Using a vegetable peeler, scrape cucumber vertically, creating alternating stripes. Trim and discard ends from cucumber. Cut cucumber into 1-inch sections, making sure cuts are straight so that cucumber sections will sit level. Turn each section onto a cut side, and place on a work surface or platter. Using a melon baller, scoop out cucumber sections, discarding center pulp, to create a cavity. Set aside.

• In a small bowl, combine sour cream, lemon zest, and salt, stirring to blend. Spoon ½ teaspoon sour cream mixture into each cucumber section.
• Cut smoked salmon into 20 elongated pieces. Arrange 2 salmon pieces in each cucumber section, folding and ruffling to fit cavity. Add a small dollop of remaining sour cream mixture to center of salmon. Top with caviar.
• Garnish with dill sprigs, if desired.

Make-Ahead Tip: *Cucumber sections can be scraped, cut, and scooped a day in advance and refrigerated in a resealable plastic bag. Sour cream mixture can be made a day in advance and refrigerated in a covered container. Assemble up to an hour in advance, and refrigerate, covered, until serving time. Garnish just before serving.*

Kitchen Tip: *To keep fresh dill from wilting, soak in ice water for 10 minutes.*

• Add chicken stock, beans, tomatoes, cumin, oregano, salt, chipotle pepper, and black pepper. Bring to a boil, stirring occasionally. When mixture reaches a boil, reduce heat to simmer. Cover, and cook for 1 hour, stirring occasionally.
• Add chicken, and cook until chicken is heated through, approximately 5 minutes.
• Serve warm.
• Garnish individual servings with cilantro, if desired.

*Mexican oregano is less sweet than regular oregano. Regular oregano may be substituted for Mexican oregano, if desired.

Make-Ahead Tip: *Refrigerate in a covered container for up to 2 days. Reheat in a saucepan over medium heat.*

Curried Tomato Soup
Gluten-free | *Yield: 8 (½-cup) servings*
Preparation: 20 minutes | *Cook: 1½ hours*

3 tablespoons olive oil
1 cup chopped red bell pepper
½ cup shallot slices
2 (28-ounce) cans peeled whole tomatoes
2 cups no-salt-added vegetable stock
1 teaspoon ground cumin
1 to 2 teaspoons curry powder
1 teaspoon ground coriander
1 teaspoon salt
½ teaspoon ground paprika
¼ teaspoon ground cinnamon
⅛ teaspoon ground cloves
⅛ teaspoon ground nutmeg
¼ teaspoon ground black pepper
Garnish: plain yogurt, toasted coconut

• In a large saucepan, heat olive oil over medium-high heat. Add bell pepper and shallot. Reduce heat to low, and cook, stirring occasionally, until vegetables are tender, approximately 10 minutes.
• Add tomatoes, breaking apart with a spoon. Add stock, cumin, curry powder to taste, coriander, salt, paprika, cinnamon, cloves, nutmeg, and pepper. Bring to a boil, and then reduce heat to a simmer. Cook for 1½ hours, stirring occasionally. Remove soup from heat.
• Using a hand-held immersion blender, purée soup mixture until smooth. Return soup to heat, and bring to a simmer.
• Serve warm.
• Garnish individual servings with yogurt and toasted coconut, if desired.

Smoky Chicken and Bean Soup
Gluten-free | *Yield: 8 to 10 servings*
Preparation: 30 minutes | *Cook: 1 hour*

1 tablespoon olive oil
1 cup chopped onion
½ cup chopped red bell pepper
½ cup chopped orange bell pepper
½ cup chopped green bell pepper
2 teaspoons finely chopped garlic
4 cups low-sodium chicken stock
2 (15.5-ounce) cans navy beans, rinsed and drained
1 cup canned petite diced tomatoes with liquid
1 teaspoon ground cumin
1 teaspoon dried Mexican oregano leaves*
½ teaspoon salt
¼ teaspoon ground chipotle pepper
¼ teaspoon ground black pepper
1½ cups chopped cooked rotisserie chicken
Garnish: chopped fresh cilantro

• In a medium stockpot, heat olive oil over medium-high heat. Add onion and bell peppers, and reduce heat to medium. Cook, stirring occasionally, until vegetables are crisp-tender, approximately 5 minutes. (Reduce heat again if vegetables start to brown too quickly.) Add garlic during last minute of cooking. Stir, and cook for 1 minute.

Lisa's Tea Treasures
Tea Room & Gift Parlour
with passion and a little hard work

Victorian-themed tearoom might seem a little out of place in California's Silicon Valley. But Dale Ann Johnson, owner of Lisa's Tea Treasures Tea Room & Gift Parlour in Campbell, believes her business serves a vital purpose in this incubator of technology.

"Silicon Valley is one of the most plugged-in, tech-savvy places in the country, if not the world," Dale Ann explains. "Everyone is busy texting, e-mailing, and Instagramming someone." Lisa's Tea Treasures provides a tranquil place where busy professionals can put their cell phones on mute and connect personally with family and friends. "It's just a place to forget about the crazy, hustle-bustle world out there."

In the late 1990s, Dale Ann's children were almost grown, and she knew she was ready to go back to work. "I knew very little about anything technology related," she says, "but I had always loved going to tea and having tea parties at my home. I thought opening a tearoom was something I would love to do." She had no experience in food service or retail sales, but tea was her passion. "With passion and a little hard work, you can make things happen," she says. In 1997, she opened Lisa's Tea Treasures Tea Room.

Eighteen years later, she says, "The best thing about owning a tearoom has been the wonderful people I have met along the way, both staff and customers. So many of them have become good friends." When customers she hasn't seen in a while come into the tearoom, it's like a homecoming. "Everybody's hugging and catching up and sharing happy times and shedding tears over sad times together," she says. "I've been so blessed."

Blackberry-Brie Chicken Salad
Gluten-free | *Yield: 8 (½-cup) servings*
Preparation: 25 minutes | *Refrigerate: 3 to 4 hours*

⅔ cup mayonnaise
½ cup sour cream
4 cups chopped cooked chicken
1½ cups toasted chopped pecans
2 to 3 tablespoons chopped fresh tarragon
½ teaspoon salt
¼ teaspoon ground black pepper
Salad greens, such as spring mix or romaine
    or a mixture of both
1 recipe Blackberry Vinaigrette (recipe follows)
Fresh or frozen blackberries
French brie cheese, cut into cubes and rind removed
Garnish: edible pansies*

• In a large bowl, combine mayonnaise and sour cream, whisking to blend. Add chicken, stirring to combine. Add pecans, tarragon, salt, and pepper. (Mixture should be creamy but not wet. If chicken salad seems dry, add more sour cream or mayonnaise as needed.)
• Cover, and refrigerate until cold, 3 to 4 hours.
• Toss salad greens with desired amount of Blackberry Vinaigrette. Divide salad greens among 8 salad plates. Place a scoop of chicken salad on each plate. Top salad greens with blackberries and cheese.
• Garnish each salad with a pansy, if desired.

Edible flowers are available from Gourmet Sweet Botanicals. To order, call 800-931-7530, or visit gourmetsweetbotanicals.com.

†*Dale Ann Johnson at Lisa's Tea Treasures uses Louis XIV's Favorite, her own house blend of Yin Ho (oolong) jasmine tea with dried blackberries, to make this recipe. To purchase, call 408-371-7377.*

Blackberry Viniagrette
Gluten-free | Yield: 2 cups | Preparation: 10 minutes

1 cup salad oil
½ cup red wine vinegar
½ cup blackberry preserves
¼ cup brewed blackberry oolong tea[†]
1 tablespoon honey
2 teaspoons sugar
2 teaspoons chopped fresh thyme

2 teaspoons chopped fresh basil
2 teaspoons Dijon-style mustard
½ teaspoon ground black pepper
¼ teaspoon salt

• In a 1-quart jar with a screw-top lid, combine oil, vinegar, blackberry preserves, tea, honey, sugar, thyme, basil, mustard, pepper, and salt. Shake well to blend.
• Refrigerate for up to 2 days until needed.

Cream of Celery Soup

Gluten-free | *Yield: 8 (½-cup) servings*
Preparation: 45 minutes | *Bake: 30 minutes*
Cook: 30 minutes

4 cups celery slices (⅛-inch slices)
2 tablespoons olive oil
4 cups chicken broth
1 cup celery leaves, packed
¼ cup heavy whipping cream
Salt to taste
Garnish: Parmesan Sourdough Croutons
   (recipe follows)

• Preheat oven to 350°.
• Line 2 baking sheets with parchment paper. Set aside.
• In a medium bowl, combine celery slices and olive oil, stirring until coated. Divide between prepared baking sheets, and spread in a single layer.
• Bake until tender, approximately 30 minutes.
• In a medium saucepan, combine broth, roasted celery, and celery leaves. Bring to a boil. Reduce heat to a brisk simmer, stirring occasionally and keeping pan covered. Cook until celery is very tender, approximately 30 minutes. Remove from heat, and let cool slightly.
• Add cream. Transfer mixture to the container of a blender, and process at high speed until very smooth and creamy. (Process in batches, if necessary.) Add salt to taste, if desired.
• Serve warm.
• Garnish individual servings with a Parmesan Sourdough Crouton, if desired.

Parmesan Sourdough Croutons
Yield: 8 croutons | *Preparation: 10 minutes* | *Bake: 5 minutes*

4 slices sourdough French bread*
1 tablespoon salted butter, softened
1 tablespoon finely grated Parmesan cheese
⅛ teaspoon ground hot paprika

• Preheat oven to 350°.
• Line a baking sheet with parchment paper. Set aside.
• Using a heart-shaped cutter, cut 8 shapes from bread slices. Place bread hearts on prepared baking sheet. Spread each bread heart with butter, and then sprinkle evenly with Parmesan cheese and paprika.
• Bake until cheese melts and bread is golden brown, approximately 5 minutes.
• Store at room temperature for up to 1 day in an airtight container until ready to serve.

To make gluten-free, replace French bread with a gluten-free bread.

Chicken Waldorf Salad

Gluten-free | *Yield: 6 (1-cup) servings*
Preparation: 20 minutes | *Refrigerate: 4 hours*

1 cup mayonnaise
1 tablespoon sugar
1 tablespoon poppy seeds
1 tablespoon fresh lemon juice
1 tablespoon champagne vinegar
1 tablespoon heavy whipping cream
¼ teaspoon salt
3 cups diced Gala apple
2 cups diced cooked chicken breast
1 cup red grape halves
⅓ cup diced celery
⅓ cup chopped toasted pecans
Garnish: Bibb lettuce

• In a small bowl, combine mayonnaise, sugar, poppy seeds, lemon juice, vinegar, cream, and salt, whisking well. Set aside.
• In a large bowl, combine apple, chicken, grape halves, celery, and pecans. Add mayonnaise mixture, tossing to coat. Cover, and refrigerate chicken salad until cold, approximately 4 hours.
• Garnish individual servings with Bibb lettuce leaves, if desired.

> *"Good manners: The noise you don't make when you're eating soup."*
>
> —Bennett Cerf

Sweet-Pea Soup

Yield: 8 (1-cup) servings | Preparation: 10 minutes
Cook: 22 to 25 minutes

1 cup thinly sliced leeks (white parts only)
5 tablespoons salted butter
5 tablespoons all-purpose flour
6 cups chicken broth
6 cups frozen baby sweet peas
⅓ cup heavy whipping cream
¼ teaspoon salt
⅛ teaspoon ground black pepper
Garnish: sour cream, fresh pea shoots

• Separate leek slices into rings, and rinse well. Pat dry.
• In a medium saucepan, melt butter over medium heat. Add leeks, and cook until soft, approximately 5 minutes.
• Add flour, whisking constantly until lightly browned, 1 to 2 minutes. Add broth, whisking to combine. Bring mixture to a boil, stirring occasionally.
• Add peas, reduce heat, and simmer for 15 minutes. Remove from heat.
• Using a hand-held immersion blender, purée soup mixture until smooth. Add cream, salt, and pepper, stirring to combine.
• Serve warm.
• Garnish individual servings with sour cream and pea shoots, if desired.

Creamy Yellow Split Pea and Sweet Potato Soup

Gluten-free | Yield: 6 (1-cup) servings
Preparation: 30 minutes | Soak: 6 to 8 hours
Cook: 2¼ hours

1 cup dried yellow split peas
2 tablespoons olive oil
½ cup chopped sweet onion
½ cup finely chopped carrot
¼ cup finely chopped celery
1 teaspoon chopped garlic
2 (32-ounce) cartons low-sodium chicken stock
2 cups cubed peeled sweet potatoes
Salt to taste
Garnish: minced smoked ham, minced fresh chives

• Soak peas in water for 6 to 8 hours. Drain, and discard water.
• In a large saucepan, heat olive oil over medium-high heat. Add onion, carrot, and celery. Reduce heat to low. Cook, stirring occasionally, until vegetables are tender, 8 to 10 minutes.
• Add garlic, and cook for 1 minute. Add stock, sweet potatoes, and soaked peas. Bring to a boil. Reduce heat to a simmer, and cook until potatoes and split peas are very tender, approximately 2 hours. Remove from heat.
• Using a hand-held immersion blender, purée soup mixture until smooth. Add salt to taste, if desired. Return to heat, and bring to a simmer.
• Serve warm.
• Garnish individual servings with minced ham and fresh chives, if desired.

Make-Ahead Tip: Refrigerate in a covered container for up to 2 days. Reheat in a saucepan over medium heat.

SECTIONING AN ORANGE

how-to on page 130

Champagne Vinaigrette
Gluten-free | *Yield: ¾ cup* | *Preparation: 5 minutes*

¼ cup champagne vinegar
1 tablespoon chopped fresh parsley
1 tablespoon chopped fresh chives
1 teaspoon sugar
¼ teaspoon kosher salt
¼ teaspoon ground black pepper
½ cup extra-virgin olive oil

• In a medium bowl, combine vinegar, parsley, chives, sugar, salt, and pepper. Whisk until sugar dissolves. Add olive oil in a slow steady stream, whisking until emulsified. Cover, and refrigerate for up to 2 days until needed.

Roasted Shrimp Cocktail
Gluten-free | *Yield: 8 servings* | *Preparation: 10 minutes*
Bake: 5 minutes | *Refrigerate: 4 hours*

24 medium shrimp, peeled, with tails on, and deveined
2 tablespoons olive oil
2 tablespoons plus 2 teaspoons fresh lemon juice, divided
¼ teaspoon salt
½ cup ketchup
2 tablespoons mayonnaise
1 teaspoon prepared grated horseradish
¼ teaspoon ground chipotle pepper
Garnish: ground chipotle pepper, parsley leaves

• Preheat oven to 400°.
• Line a rimmed baking sheet with parchment paper. Set aside.
• In a medium bowl, toss shrimp with olive oil and 2 tablespoons lemon juice. Place on prepared baking sheet in a single layer. Sprinkle with salt.
• Bake until shrimp are pink and firm to the touch, approximately 5 minutes.
• Transfer shrimp to an airtight container, and refrigerate until cold, 4 to 8 hours.
• In a small bowl, combine ketchup, mayonnaise, horseradish, chipotle pepper, and remaining 2 teaspoons lemon juice, whisking well.
• Cover, and refrigerate until cold, 4 to 24 hours.
• Divide ketchup mixture among 8 mini flared glasses.
• Garnish with chipotle pepper and parsley leaves, if desired.
• Place 3 shrimp on the edge of each glass. (Cut a small slit in the underside of shrimp, if necessary, to balance.)
• Serve immediately.

Seared Sea-Scallop Salad
Gluten-free | *Yield: 4 to 6 servings*
Preparation: 15 minutes | *Cook: 4 to 6 minutes*

¼ cup olive oil
¼ cup salted butter
12 sea scallops
Kosher salt
Ground black pepper
1 (5-ounce) bag watercress
2 blood oranges, sectioned
½ cup thinly shaved fennel
½ cup niçoise olives, pitted
¼ cup thinly sliced radishes
1 recipe Champagne Vinaigrette (recipe follows)

• In a large nonstick skillet, heat olive oil and butter over medium-high heat. Add scallops. Cook until golden brown, 2 to 3 minutes per side. Season to taste with salt and pepper. Set aside and keep warm.
• In a small bowl, combine watercress, orange sections, fennel, olives, radishes, and 3 tablespoons Champagne Vinaigrette. Toss gently to coat.
• Divide watercress mixture evenly among salad plates. Top each serving with 2 to 3 scallops.
• Serve immediately with additional vinaigrette on the side, if desired.

Quiches & Tartlets

FRESH HERB AND
GRUYÈRE QUICHE
(recipe on page 63)

Mushroom, Beef, and Asparagus Puff Pastry Boxes

Yield: 8 tartlets | *Preparation: 45 minutes*
Bake: 16 to 18 minutes | *Cool: 30 minutes* | *Cook: 5 minutes*

1 (17.5-ounce) package frozen puff pastry
  (2 sheets), slightly thawed
1 large egg
1 tablespoon water
24 stalks thin fresh asparagus
½ teaspoon olive oil
¾ cup chopped dried beef, such as Armour
6 tablespoons salted butter, divided
1 (8-ounce) carton whole baby portobello mushrooms,
  thinly sliced
3 tablespoons all-purpose flour

1¾ cup beef stock
1 tablespoon dry sherry
1 teaspoon Worcestershire sauce
¼ teaspoon garlic powder
¼ teaspoon ground black pepper
1 teaspoon fresh thyme leaves

• Preheat oven to 400°.
• Line a rimmed baking sheet with parchment paper.
Set aside.
• On a lightly floured surface, unfold puff pastry. Using
a 2¾-inch square cutter, cut 16 squares from puff pastry
sheets. Using a 2-inch square cutter, cut and remove
centers from 8 squares to create frames, discarding center squares. Stack 1 frame on top of each solid square.
Place stacks 2 inches apart on prepared baking sheet.

- In a small bowl, combine egg and water, whisking well. Lightly brush egg mixture over tops of puff pastry frames.
- Bake until golden brown, approximately 11 minutes. Let cool completely. Store in an airtight container until ready to fill.
- Line another rimmed baking sheet with parchment paper. Place asparagus on prepared baking sheet, and drizzle with olive oil.
- Bake until asparagus is just tender when pierced with the tip of a sharp knife, 5 to 7 minutes. (Asparagus should be bright green.) Let cool completely.
- Cut 3 inches from tops of asparagus, reserving for garnish. Chop remaining asparagus stalks, and set aside.
- In a small bowl, soak dried beef slices in enough very hot water to cover until needed.
- In a large nonstick sauté pan, heat 2 tablespoons butter over medium-high heat. Add mushrooms, reduce heat to medium, and cook, stirring occasionally, until mushrooms are tender, approximately 5 minutes. Remove mushrooms, and set aside.
- In the same pan, melt remaining 4 tablespoons butter over medium-high heat. Reduce heat to medium, add flour, whisking and cooking for 3 minutes until a smooth paste forms. Add beef stock, sherry, Worcestershire sauce, garlic powder, and pepper, cooking over low heat and whisking until sauce is smooth.
- Drain beef well, and add to sauce. Add thyme, mushrooms, and asparagus, cooking and stirring until heated through.
- Divide warm mushroom mixture evenly among puff pastry boxes. Arrange 3 asparagus tips diagonally over filling.
- Serve immediately.

Tapenade and Cream Cheese Tartlets

Yield: 16 tartlets | Preparation: 45 minutes
Bake: 8 to 10 minutes

1 cup green pimiento-stuffed olives
¼ cup pitted black olives, such as kalamata
1 small clove garlic
2 tablespoons chopped fresh basil
2 tablespoons chopped fresh parsley
1 tablespoon olive oil
1 teaspoon fresh lemon juice
½ teaspoon fresh thyme leaves
1 (17.5-ounce) package frozen puff pastry
    (2 sheets), slightly thawed
3 ounces cream cheese, softened
1 teaspoon fresh lemon zest
½ teaspoon heavy whipping cream
1 large egg
1 tablespoon water

- Preheat oven to 400°.
- Line a rimmed baking sheet with parchment paper. Set aside.
- In the work bowl of a food processor, combine green olives, black olives, garlic, basil, parsley, olive oil, lemon juice, and thyme. Pulse until olives are finely chopped. Set aside.
- On a lightly floured surface, unfold puff pastry. Using a 1½-inch square cutter, cut 48 squares from puff pastry sheets. Using a 1-inch round cutter, cut and remove center circles from 32 squares to create frames, discarding center circles. Stack 2 frames on top of each solid square. Place stacks 2 inches apart on prepared baking sheet. Set aside.
- In a small mixing bowl, combine cream cheese, lemon zest, and cream. Beat at medium speed with a mixer until well blended. Transfer cream cheese mixture to a piping bag or a resealable plastic bag with a corner snipped off. Pipe cream cheese mixture evenly into cavity of each puff pastry stack.
- In a small bowl, combine egg and water, whisking well. Lightly brush egg mixture over tops of puff pastry frames.
- Bake until puff pastry is golden brown, 8 to 10 minutes. Let cool slightly.
- Using a finger or a small spoon, press cream cheese centers down into wells. Fill each tartlet with a small amount of tapenade.
- Serve warm or at room temperature.

- In a large bowl, combine eggs, cheese, chives, salt, and pepper, whisking well. Set aside.
- Layer asparagus in prepared baking pan. Pour egg mixture evenly over asparagus.
- Bake until set, 15 to 20 minutes. Let cool in pan for 10 minutes.
- Turn quiche out onto a cutting board. Cut into 18 (3-x-1½-inch) rectangles. Wrap each rectangle with a prosciutto strip.
- Garnish each piece with a chive length, if desired.
- Serve immediately.

Arugula, Lemon, and Gruyère Quiche

Yield: 1 (9-inch) quiche (approximately 8 servings)
Preparation: 20 minutes | Refrigerate: 30 minutes
Bake: 38 to 40 minutes | Cool: 20 minutes

½ (14.1-ounce) package refrigerated pie dough
   (1 sheet)
4 cups arugula
3 large eggs
1½ cups heavy whipping cream
1 tablespoon fresh lemon zest
½ teaspoon salt
¼ teaspoon ground black pepper
¼ teaspoon ground nutmeg
2 cups coarsely shredded Gruyère cheese

- Preheat oven to 450°.
- Lightly spray a 9-inch tart pan with a removable bottom with cooking spray. Unroll pie dough, and press into bottom and up sides of prepared tart pan, trimming and discarding excess dough. Refrigerate for 30 minutes.
- Prick bottom of pie dough with a fork to prevent puffing while baking.
- Bake for 5 minutes. Let cool completely.
- Reduce oven temperature to 350°.
- Place arugula in a colander, and rinse with water.
- Heat a large nonstick sauté pan over high heat. Add wet arugula, stirring and tossing just until wilted and tender, approximately 1 minute. Place arugula in a bowl to cool, and squeeze out excess liquid. Chop finely. Set aside.
- In a medium bowl, combine eggs, cream, lemon zest, salt, pepper, and nutmeg, whisking until blended. Set aside.
- Sprinkle cheese into baked tart shell. Arrange arugula evenly over cheese. Pour egg mixture over arugula. Bake until quiche is slightly puffed and lightly browned, 38 to 40 minutes. Let cool for 15 minutes before removing from tart pan and serving.

Asparagus-Prosciutto Crustless Quiche

Gluten-free | Yield: 18 pieces | Preparation: 20 minutes
Bake: 15 to 20 minutes | Cool: 10 minutes

1 pound thin to medium asparagus
6 large eggs
¼ cup grated Parmesan cheese
2 tablespoons minced chives
½ teaspoon salt
½ teaspoon freshly ground black pepper
6 slices prosciutto, each cut into 3 long strips
Garnish: 18 (2-inch-long) chives

- Preheat oven to 400°.
- Line a 9-inch square baking pan with parchment paper. Set aside.
- Trim asparagus spears to 8 inches in length, discarding tough ends.
- In a large sauté pan, bring 2 inches water to a boil. Immerse asparagus in boiling water for 1 minute to blanch. Transfer asparagus to an ice-water bath to stop the cooking process. Drain asparagus and pat dry. Set aside.

The English Rose Tea Room
a proper cup of tea

Jo Gemmill, owner of the English Rose Tea Room, is not ashamed to admit that she opened her tearoom for a very selfish reason—she was homesick. The Hampshire, England, native married an American 17 years ago and moved to the United States. "I wanted to surround myself with familiar things and have a cup of tea whenever I wanted," she says. "I found a place to rent at the corner of Lucky Lane and Easy Street in Carefree, Arizona. It sounded like a good omen."

The tearoom serves afternoon tea, as well as a full lunch menu. "Everything is made in-house," Jo points out. "We have all sorts of lovely things on the menu—from scones and English trifle right through to ploughman's lunches and that good old British staple, beans on toast."

The one thing you are guaranteed to find at The English Rose is a proper British cup of tea. That, Jo says, is 1) hot—preferably boiling hot, 2) strong, and 3) served with milk. "I have a huge tea menu—more than 50 different teas. My main purveyors are Harney & Sons and Taylors of Harrogate." Every tea served in the tearoom is available for purchase in the gift shop.

"We have a very strong connection with the British royal family," Jo adds. "We have celebrated every significant royal event that has happened over the last 15 years." That includes the royal wedding of Prince William and Catherine Middleton, baby showers for Prince George and Princess Charlotte, and the Queen's Diamond Jubilee. A special treat for the tearoom's guests is having their photograph made with the Queen. "We have a life-size cardboard cutout of the Queen in the tearoom," Jo explains. "She's the most photographed piece of cardboard in Carefree."

Smoked Salmon Quiche
Yield: 1 (9-inch) quiche (approximately 8 servings)
Preparation: 20 minutes | Bake: 45 minutes

4 large eggs
1 cup heavy whipping cream
¼ teaspoon ground black pepper
1¾ cups shredded sharp Cheddar cheese, divided
8 ounces smoked salmon, chopped
1 tablespoon dried minced onion
1 unbaked frozen 9-inch deep-dish pie shell, such as Marie Callender's, thawed

• Preheat oven to 350°.
• In a large bowl, combine eggs, cream, and pepper, whisking to blend. Set aside.
• In another bowl, combine 1½ cups cheese, salmon, and onion, stirring gently. Spread salmon mixture into pie shell. Pour egg mixture over salmon mixture. Sprinkle remaining ¼ cup cheese over egg mixture. Place pie pan on a baking sheet.
• Bake quiche on center rack of oven until firm, 35 to 45 minutes.
• Let cool slightly before serving.

Broccoli Quiche Squares

Gluten-free variation | *Yield: 24 servings*
Preparation: 25 minutes | *Bake: 35 minutes* | *Cool: 1 hour*

½ teaspoon olive oil
¼ cup finely chopped orange bell pepper
2 cups coarsely shredded Gruyère cheese
2 cups cooked fresh broccoli florets, finely chopped
5 large eggs
2 cups heavy whipping cream
½ teaspoon salt
¼ teaspoon ground black pepper
24 square wheat crackers, such as Wheat Thins
    BIG Crackers*

• Preheat oven to 350°.
• Spray a shallow 13-x-9-inch baking pan with cooking spray. Set aside.
• In a small nonstick skillet, heat olive oil over medium-high heat. Add bell pepper, and cook until tender, 1 to 2 minutes. Set aside.
• Sprinkle 1 cup cheese into prepared baking pan. Scatter broccoli and bell pepper over cheese. Sprinkle remaining 1 cup cheese over vegetables. Set aside.
• In a medium bowl, combine eggs, cream, salt, and black pepper, whisking well. Pour over cheese and vegetables in baking pan.
• Bake until quiche is set and slightly puffed, approximately 30 minutes. Let cool completely.
• Line a baking sheet with parchment paper. Set aside.
• Using a 1½-inch square cutter, cut 24 squares from quiche. Place each quiche square on a cracker. Place squares on prepared baking sheet.
• Heat in oven until warm, approximately 5 minutes.
• Serve immediately.

For a gluten-free version of this recipe, replace wheat crackers with gluten-free crackers, or serve without crackers.

Ham and Chive Quiches

Yield: 8 (4-inch) quiches | *Preparation: 15 minutes*
Refrigerate: 30 minutes | *Bake: 22 to 25 minutes*
Cool: 30 minutes

1 (14.1-ounce) package refrigerated pie dough
    (2 sheets)
1 cup diced smoked ham (¼-inch cubes)
1 cup coarsely shredded fontina cheese
3 large eggs
1¼ cups heavy whipping cream
½ teaspoon salt
⅛ teaspoon ground black pepper
2 teaspoons chopped fresh chives

• Preheat oven to 450°.
• On a lightly floured surface, unroll pie dough. Using a 4½-inch round cutter, cut 8 circles from dough. Lightly spray 8 (4-inch) tartlet pans with cooking spray. Press dough rounds into tartlet pans, trimming excess as necessary. Using the large end of a chopstick, press dough into indentations in sides of tartlet pans.
• Place tartlet pans on a rimmed baking sheet. Refrigerate for 30 minutes.
• Prick bottom of pie dough with a fork to prevent puffing while baking.
• Bake until light golden brown, 7 to 8 minutes. Let cool completely before filling.
• Reduce oven temperature to 350°.
• In a small nonstick sauté pan, sear ham over medium-high heat until very lightly browned.
• Place 1 tablespoon ham and 2 tablespoons cheese in each prepared tartlet pan. Set aside.
• In a large liquid-measuring cup, combine eggs, cream, salt, and pepper, whisking well. Divide egg mixture evenly among tartlet pans. Sprinkle each quiche with ¼ teaspoon chives.
• Bake until quiches are set and slightly puffed, 15 to 18 minutes. Let cool slightly before removing from tartlet pans.
• Serve warm or at room temperature for up to 3 hours.

Make-Ahead Tip: Quiches can be baked a day in advance and stored in a covered container in the refrigerator. Reheat on a rimmed baking sheet in a 350° oven for 6 to 8 minutes.

TARTLET
CRUST

*how-to on
page 128*

TARTLET
CRUST
*how-to on
page 128*

Tomato-Feta Tartlets

Yield: 8 (4½-x-2½-inch) tartlets | Preparation: 25 minutes
Refrigerate: 30 minutes | Bake: 15 minutes
Cool: 30 minutes

1 (14.1-ounce) package refrigerated pie dough
   (2 sheets)
½ cup mayonnaise
½ cup plus 2 tablespoons crumbled feta cheese,
   divided
2 tablespoons chopped fresh basil
¼ teaspoon ground black pepper
1 cup red grape tomatoes
1 cup yellow grape tomatoes
Garnish: fresh basil

• Preheat oven to 450°.
• On a lightly floured surface, unroll pie dough. Using a 4½-x-2½-inch tartlet pan as a guide, cut 8 shapes from dough. Lightly spray 8 tartlet pans with cooking spray. Press dough shapes into prepared tartlet pans, trimming excess as necessary. Using the large end of a chopstick, press dough into indentations in sides of tartlet pans.
• Place tartlet pans on a rimmed baking sheet. Refrigerate for 30 minutes.
• Prick tartlet dough with a fork to prevent puffing during baking.
• Bake for 5 minutes. Let cool completely.
• Reduce oven temperature to 350°.
• In a small bowl, combine mayonnaise, ½ cup cheese, basil, and pepper, stirring to blend. Divide mayonnaise mixture evenly among prepared tartlet shells, spreading evenly.
• Cut tomatoes in half lengthwise. Divide tomato halves evenly among prepared tartlet shells, and arrange vertically in a shingled fashion. Sprinkle remaining 2 tablespoons cheese over tomatoes.
• Bake tartlets until tomatoes have softened and are tender, approximately 10 minutes. When cool enough to handle, remove from tartlet pans.
• Serve warm or at room temperature.
• Garnish each with fresh basil, if desired.

Make-Ahead Tip: *Tartlet shells can be made earlier in the day and stored in an airtight container until needed.*

Smoked Salmon Croustades

Yield: 24 mini tartlets | Preparation: 45 minutes

1 (8-ounce) package cream cheese, softened
2 tablespoons finely chopped fresh dill
2 teaspoons fresh lemon zest
2 teaspoons fresh lemon juice
¼ teaspoon salt
¼ teaspoon ground black pepper
24 mini croustades, such as Siljans
2 (4-ounce) packages thinly sliced smoked salmon,
   such as Echo Falls
Garnish: fresh dill

• In a medium mixing bowl, combine cream cheese, dill, lemon zest, lemon juice, salt, and pepper. Beat at high speed with a mixer until well blended.
• Transfer cream cheese mixture to a piping bag fitted with a medium open-star tip (Wilton #21). Pipe enough mixture into each croustade to cover bottom in an even layer. Set aside.
• Cut smoked salmon into ¾-inch strips of varying lengths, but no longer than 2 inches. Arrange salmon strips in concentric circles in each croustade to form a rose.
• Pipe a cream cheese rosette into center of each salmon rose.
• Garnish each croustade with a fresh dill sprig, if desired.

Make-Ahead Tip: *Cheese mixture can be made a day in advance and refrigerated in a covered container until needed. For ease of piping, let soften before using. Croustades can be assembled an hour in advance and stored, covered, in the refrigerator. Garnish just before serving.*

The Secret Garden
Tea Room & Gift Shop
mystery solved

Nancy Drew's adventures in the famous mystery series inspired young readers to dream of becoming detectives, but the beloved heroine led Elizabeth Kleingartner of The Secret Garden in Sumner, Washington, down a different path.

Nancy and her friends often stopped at tearooms on the way to their next adventure. Thus began Elizabeth's love affair with the ritual of tea. She cataloged her experiences, and in the pages of a small notebook, built a menu and sketched a plan for the tearoom.

Elizabeth opened The Secret Garden Gift Shop in Bellevue, Washington, in 1989, and over the next 13 years, the business steadily grew. Then in 2002, the shop hosted a one-time Mother's Day tea. Response was so enthusiastic, Elizabeth decided to act on her dreams. The Secret Garden Tea Room opened in November of that same year.

Three years later, Elizabeth and husband Mark, the tearoom's head chef, were looking for a larger location for The Secret Garden, preferably in a nearby shopping center. But a photo a real estate agent showed them of a Victorian mansion in Sumner, just 35 minutes south, piqued their interest.

"We thought we'd just come look at a neat old house," Mark says. "We fell in love with it and decided to find a way to make it work."

The years since that first Mother's Day tea have been eventful, and Elizabeth says she is most proud of the tearoom's lasting impact. "We get to be a part of special times—weddings, anniversaries, milestone birthdays, and baby showers."

Caramelized Walla Walla Sweet Onion Cups

Yield: 32 tartlets | Preparation: 30 minutes
Cook: 20 minutes | Bake: 12 minutes

2 large sweet onions, such as Walla Walla
2 tablespoons olive oil
½ teaspoon dried thyme
1 tablespoon brown sugar
1 tablespoon balsamic vinegar
4 ounces cream cheese, softened
4 ounces goat cheese, at room temperature
¼ teaspoon ground black pepper
⅛ teaspoon salt
2 (17.5-ounce) packages puff pastry (4 sheets), thawed
Garnish: fresh thyme sprigs

• Preheat oven to 375°.
• Cut onions in half from root to stem, and thinly slice.
• In a large stockpot, heat olive oil over medium heat. Add onions and thyme. Cook, stirring occasionally, until onions are quite soft and begin to darken. Add brown sugar and vinegar, and cook, stirring occasionally, until onions are caramel colored.
• Add cream cheese and goat cheese. Reduce heat. Cook, stirring often, until cheeses melt completely. Add pepper and salt, stirring to incorporate. Let mixture cool in refrigerator.
• Lightly spray 32 wells of mini muffin pans with cooking spray. Set aside.
• On a lightly floured surface, unfold puff pastry. Cut 32 (2½-inch) squares from dough. Press squares into prepared wells of mini muffin pans, flaring corners of pastry upward. Divide onion mixture among prepared wells of muffin pans.
• Bake until puff pastry is golden, approximately 12 minutes.
• Serve warm.
• Garnish each tartlet with a sprig of fresh thyme, if desired.

TARTLET
CRUST

*how-to on
page 128*

Kale and Sausage Quiches

Yield: 12 (4-inch) quiches | Preparation: 45 minutes
Refrigerate: 30 minutes | Bake: 22 to 25 minutes
Cool: 30 minutes

1 (14.1-ounce) package refrigerated pie dough
    (2 sheets)
1 tablespoon olive oil
3 cups coarsely chopped curly kale
¾ cup shredded fontina cheese
¾ cup grated Parmesan cheese
¾ cup crumbled, cooked pork breakfast sausage
3 large eggs
1 cup heavy whipping cream
¼ teaspoon salt
¼ teaspoon ground black pepper
⅛ teaspoon ground nutmeg

• Preheat oven to 450°.
• On a lightly floured surface, unroll pie dough. Using a 4½-inch round cutter, cut 12 circles from dough. Lightly spray 12 (4-inch) tartlet pans with cooking spray. Press dough rounds into tartlet pans, trimming excess as necessary. Using the large end of a chopstick, press dough into indentations in sides of tartlet pans.
• Place tartlet pans on a rimmed baking sheet. Refrigerate for 30 minutes.
• Prick bottom of pie dough with a fork to prevent puffing while baking.
• Bake until light golden brown, 7 to 8 minutes. Let cool completely before filling.
• Reduce oven temperature to 350°.
• In a medium sauté pan, heat olive oil over medium-high heat until oil shimmers. Add kale, and cook until wilted and tender. Let cool.
• In each prepared tartlet pan, layer 1 tablespoon each fontina cheese, Parmesan cheese, sausage, and kale. Set aside.
• In a large liquid-measuring cup, combine eggs, cream, salt, pepper, and nutmeg, whisking well. Divide egg mixture evenly among tartlet pans.
• Bake until quiches are set and slightly puffed, 15 to 18 minutes. Let cool slightly before removing from tartlet pans.
• Serve warm or at room temperature for up to 3 hours.

Make-Ahead Tip: Quiches can be baked a day in advance and stored in a covered container in the refrigerator. Reheat on a rimmed baking sheet in a 350° oven for 6 to 8 minutes.

Apricot-Chive Chicken Salad in Puff Pastry Shells

Yield: 8 servings | Preparation: 15 minutes

2 cups chopped cooked chicken
½ cup chopped dried apricots
2 tablespoons toasted slivered almonds
1 tablespoon chopped fresh chives
¾ cup mayonnaise
1 tablespoon lemon juice
¼ teaspoon salt
⅛ teaspoon ground black pepper
8 frozen puff pastry shells, such as Pepperidge Farm, thawed and baked according to package directions
Garnish: apricot roses*, fresh chives

• In a large bowl, combine chicken, apricots, almonds, chives, mayonnaise, lemon juice, salt, and pepper, stirring well. Cover, and refrigerate until just before serving.
• Divide chicken salad evenly among puff pastry shells.
• Garnish with an apricot rose and a chive, if desired.
• Serve immediately.

*To make apricot roses, slice dried apricots lengthwise into thin slices. Roll slices into rosettes.

Make-Ahead Tip: Apricot-Chive Chicken Salad can be made a day in advance and refrigerated until needed. Add almonds just before serving.

TARTLET CRUST
how-to on page 128

• In a small bowl, combine lobster, mayonnaise, lemon juice, celery, onion, and salt, tossing until mixed. Cover, and refrigerate until cold, 3 to 4 hours.
• Preheat oven to 450°.
• On a lightly floured surface, unroll pie dough. Using a 4½-x-1½-inch barquette tartlet pan as a guide, cut 6 shapes from dough. Lightly spray 6 tartlet pans with cooking spray. Press dough shapes into prepared tartlet pans, trimming excess as necessary. Using the large end of a chopstick, press dough into indentations in sides of tartlet pans.
• Place tartlet pans on a rimmed baking sheet. Refrigerate for 30 minutes.
• Prick tartlet dough with a fork to prevent puffing during baking.
• Bake until golden brown, 7 to 9 minutes. Let cool on wire racks. Carefully remove tartlet shells from pans.
• When ready to serve, divide lobster salad among prepared tartlet shells.
• Garnish each with a lemon peel curl, if desired.

Spinach-Artichoke Phyllo Cups

Yield: 30 mini tartlets | Preparation: 15 minutes
Cook: 1 to 2 minutes | Bake: 10 to 12 minutes

1 teaspoon olive oil
1 (6-ounce) bag fresh baby spinach
¼ cup finely chopped canned artichoke hearts
3 tablespoons mayonnaise, such as Hellman's
2 tablespoons sour cream
⅔ cup freshly finely grated Parmesan cheese
⅛ teaspoon garlic salt
⅛ teaspoon ground black pepper
⅛ teaspoon ground red pepper
2 (1.9-ounce) boxes frozen mini phyllo cups
    (30 phyllo cups), such as Athens, thawed

• Preheat oven to 350°.
• In a large nonstick sauté pan, heat olive oil over medium-high heat. Add spinach, stirring until wilted and tender, 1 to 2 minutes.
• Transfer spinach to a bowl. Using kitchen scissors, cut spinach into small pieces. Drain any remaining liquid.
• To spinach, add artichokes, mayonnaise, sour cream, Parmesan cheese, garlic salt, black pepper, and red pepper, stirring to combine. Evenly divide spinach mixture among phyllo cups. Place filled phyllo cups on a rimmed baking sheet.
• Bake until filling is hot and cheese melts, 10 to 12 minutes.
• Serve immediately.

Lobster Salad Barquettes

Yield: 6 (4½-x-1½-inch) tartlets | Preparation: 30 minutes
Cook: 7 to 8 minutes | Refrigerate: 3½ to 4½ hours
Bake: 7 to 9 minutes | Cool: 30 minutes

3 (5-ounce) lobster tails
1 cup water
1 tablespoon salt
2 tablespoons mayonnaise, such as Hellman's
2 tablespoons fresh lemon juice
2 tablespoons minced celery
1 tablespoon minced red onion
⅛ teaspoon salt
½ (14.1-ounce) package refrigerated pie dough
    (1 sheet)
Garnish: lemon peel curls

• Insert a skewer lengthwise along top of each lobster tail to prevent curling during steaming. Set aside.
• In a medium saucepan with a steamer basket, bring water and salt to a boil. Place prepared lobster tails in steamer basket, and steam, covered, until shells turn pink and meat is opaque white, 7 to 8 minutes. Remove lobster tails from steamer, and let cool slightly until cool enough to handle.
• Using kitchen scissors, cut lobster tails along back of shell, pull open, and remove lobster meat. Chop meat into ½-inch pieces.

Miss Tami's Tea Cottage
an accidental tearoom

When Tami Shoemaker opened her business in Meridian, Idaho, more than 25 years ago, she didn't intend to make it a full-service restaurant. In 1989, she and her husband purchased a 1912 vintage house on Main Street, remodeling the two front rooms into a gift shop and planning to raise their two boys in the rest of the house. Tami took consignments and made most of the gifts herself. But she loved to cook, and in the back of her mind, she admits, she thought about having a little corner where guests could enjoy tea and pastries.

"We were so busy," Tami recalls. "I knew I could take the business in this direction." So the Shoemakers decided to find another place to live and take a leap of faith transforming the business into a tearoom. "It was very simple. We served sandwiches, teas, and coffees."

Five years later, Tami resolved to take another huge step and install a commercial kitchen. Miss Tami's became a restaurant that serves both lunch and afternoon tea, with a Saturday brunch buffet. At teatime, guests may choose a cream tea, a cottage tea, or a full afternoon tea, served with a pot of tea.

"Owning a tea room is not something you do to get rich," Tami explains. "It's a way of life, and I enjoy it." There were a few times during the recent recession when Tami did not pay herself, but everything has worked out. "We have been so blessed," she says.

Guests keep coming back to Miss Tami's for the relaxing atmosphere and the friendly staff, some of whom have been with the Shoemakers for 18 years. And Tami returns the compliment: "They're not just my guests; they're my friends. It's all summed up when people walk through the door, take a deep breath, and say, 'What smells so good in here?'"

"That's everything," Tami says.

Basil-Anise Cheesecake Tartlets

Yield: 48 tartlets | Preparation: 20 minutes
Bake: 8 to 10 minutes | Cool: 30 minutes
Refrigerate: 2 hours

1 (8-ounce) package cream cheese, softened
3½ teaspoons sugar
2 tablespoons unsalted butter, softened
2 tablespoons all-purpose flour
2 tablespoons heavy whipping cream
1 tablespoon finely chopped fresh basil
¼ teaspoon anise seed
1 pinch fine sea salt
1 egg
2 (6.3-ounce) packages 1¾-inch shortbread tartlet
   shells, such as Clearbrook Farms (48 tartlet shells)
Garnish: fresh basil leaves

• Preheat oven to 325°.
• Arrange tartlet shells on 2 rimmed baking sheets. Set aside.
• In a large mixing bowl, combine cream cheese, sugar, and butter. Beat at high speed with a mixer fitted with a whip attachment. Add flour, cream, basil, anise, and salt, beating until smooth.
• In a separate bowl, lightly beat egg. Add egg to cream cheese mixture, beating well.
• Divide cream cheese mixture evenly among tartlet shells (approximately ¾ teaspoon per shell).
• Bake until cheesecake centers are almost set, 8 to 10 minutes. Let cool on a wire rack.
• Refrigerate for 2 hours before serving.
• Serve cold.
• Garnish each cheesecake with basil leaves, if desired.

• Remove tartlets from pan, and place on a rimmed baking sheet.
• Preheat oven to 350°.
• Warm tartlets in oven for 5 to 8 minutes.
• Meanwhile, in a nonstick skillet, heat olive oil and remaining 1½ tablespoons butter over medium-high heat. Add mushrooms. Season with remaining ¼ teaspoon salt and remaining ¼ teaspoon pepper. Cook for 5 minutes without stirring. Stir mushrooms to sear all sides. Remove from pan, and drain on paper towels.
• Top warm tartlets with hot mushrooms.
• Serve immediately.

Fresh Herb and Gruyère Quiche
Yield: 1 (9-inch) quiche (approximately 8 servings)
Preparation: 45 minutes | Refrigerate: 30 minutes
Bake: 25 minutes | Cool: 20 minutes

½ (14.1-ounce) package refrigerated pie dough (1 sheet)
1 cup coarsely shredded Gruyère cheese
2 tablespoons finely chopped fresh dill
2 tablespoons finely chopped fresh chives
1 tablespoon fresh thyme leaves
3 large eggs
1 cup heavy whipping cream
¼ teaspoon salt
¼ teaspoon ground black pepper

• Preheat oven to 450°
• Lightly spray a 9-inch tart pan with a removable bottom (or a 9-inch pie plate) with cooking spray. Unroll pie dough, and press into bottom and up sides of prepared tart pan, trimming and discarding excess dough. Refrigerate for 30 minutes.
• Prick bottom of pie dough with a fork to prevent puffing while baking.
• Bake until light golden brown, 5 to 7 minutes. Let cool completely before filling.
• Spread cheese in bottom of cooled crust. Sprinkle evenly with dill, chives, and thyme. Set aside.
• In a medium mixing bowl, combine eggs, cream, salt, and pepper, whisking well. Pour egg mixture over cheese and herbs in tart pan.
• Bake until quiche is set, approximately 25 minutes. Let cool slightly before removing from pan.
• Serve warm.

Kitchen Tip: Gruyère is more expensive than Swiss cheese but well worth the extra money. It provides a rich nutty flavor that Swiss cheeses do not.

Mushroom and Three-Cheese Tartlets
Yield: 12 tartlets | Preparation: 30 minutes
Bake: 50 minutes | Cook: 10 to 12 minutes
Cool: 1 hour | Refrigerate: 2 hours

1¾ cups finely chopped toasted pecans
1¾ cups crumbled round buttery crackers
7½ tablespoons butter, divided
1 large egg white
1 (10-ounce) package goat cheese, at room temperature
1 (8-ounce) package cream cheese, softened
1½ cups heavy whipping cream
3 large eggs
2 cups shredded Swiss cheese
1 tablespoon all-purpose flour
¾ teaspoon kosher salt, divided
½ teaspoon ground black pepper, divided
1½ tablespoons olive oil
4 cups assorted wild mushrooms, cleaned and trimmed

• Preheat oven to 325°.
• In a medium bowl, combine pecans, crackers, 6 tablespoons butter, and egg white, stirring well. Press into bottoms of a 12-well mini cheesecake pan.
• Bake for 10 minutes. Let cool completely in pan on a wire rack.
• In a large bowl, combine goat cheese and cream cheese. Beat at medium speed with a mixer until smooth. Add cream, beating to combine. Add eggs, one at time, beating well after each addition. Add Swiss cheese, flour, ½ teaspoon salt, and ¼ teaspoon pepper. Divide batter evenly among prepared wells of pan.
• Bake until set, approximately 20 minutes. Let cool in pan for 30 minutes. Refrigerate for at least 2 hours.

Kitchen Tip: To remove quiche from bottom of tart pan, use a cake lifter or a wide thin-bladed spatula.

Coq au Vin Tartlets

Yield: 8 (4½-x-2½-inch) tartlets | Preparation: 30 minutes
Refrigerate: 30 minutes | Bake: 7 minutes
Cool: 30 minutes | Cook: approximately 5 minutes

1 (14.1-ounce) package refrigerated pie dough
   (2 sheets)
½ cup sliced white button mushrooms
1 teaspoon olive oil
¼ teaspoon dried thyme

⅛ teaspoon salt
⅛ teaspoon ground black pepper
½ cup pearl onions
2 tablespoons salted butter
2 tablespoons all-purpose flour
1 cup beef stock
2 tablespoons red wine
1 tablespoon finely chopped cooked bacon
½ cup chopped roasted chicken
Garnish: fresh thyme

- Preheat oven to 450°.
- On a lightly floured surface, unroll pie dough. Using a 4½-x-2½-inch tartlet pan as a guide, cut 8 shapes from dough. Lightly spray 8 tartlet pans with cooking spray. Press dough shapes into prepared tartlet pans, trimming excess as necessary. Using the large end of a chopstick, press dough into indentations in sides of tartlet pans.
- Place tartlet pans on a rimmed baking sheet. Refrigerate for 30 minutes.
- Prick tartlet dough with a fork to prevent puffing during baking.
- Bake until edges are golden brown, 5 to 7 minutes. Let cool completely before removing from pans.
- Reduce oven temperature to 350°.
- In a small bowl, combine mushrooms, olive oil, thyme, salt, and pepper, tossing to coat. On another rimmed baking sheet, spread mushrooms in a single layer.
- Bake until mushrooms are tender and release their juices, approximately 20 minutes. Set aside.
- In a medium sauce pan, bring 2 inches water to a boil. Immerse pearl onions in boiling water for 1 minute to blanch. Transfer onions to an ice-water bath to stop the cooking process. Drain onions and pat dry. Set aside.
- In a small sauté pan, melt butter over medium-high heat. Add flour, whisking constantly. Cook until a smooth paste forms, 1 to 2 minutes, reducing heat if mixture starts to brown. Add beef stock, whisking and cooking over medium-low heat until mixture is smooth and creamy. Add wine and bacon, stirring to incorporate. Add chicken, pearl onions, and roasted mushrooms, stirring to combine and cooking until heated through, 2 to 3 minutes. Spoon chicken mixture into cooled tartlet shells.
- Garnish each with a sprinkle of fresh thyme leaves and a thyme sprig, if desired.
- Serve immediately.

Make-Ahead Tip: *Tartlet shells, roasted mushrooms, and beef gravy may be made a day in advance. Store tartlet shells in an airtight container at room temperature. Refrigerate mushrooms and gravy in separate airtight containers. Reheat gravy over low heat before adding remaining ingredients. If gravy is too thick, add more beef stock to thin.*

Apricot, Pecan, and Brie Phyllo Cups

Yield: 15 mini tartlets | Preparation: 10 minutes
Bake: 9 to 11 minutes

15 pecan halves
1 teaspoon olive oil
⅛ teaspoon salt
⅛ teaspoon ground red pepper
4 ounces Brie cheese, rind removed
1 (1.9-ounce) box frozen mini phyllo cups
    (15 phyllo cups), such as Athens, thawed
3 teaspoons apricot jam

- Preheat oven to 350°.
- In a small bowl, combine pecans and olive oil, tossing to coat. Place pecans right side up on a rimmed baking sheet. Sprinkle evenly with salt and red pepper.
- Bake until lightly toasted, 4 to 5 minutes. Let cool completely. Chop finely. Set aside.
- Divide Brie evenly among phyllo cups. Top each evenly with jam. Place filled phyllo cups on a rimmed baking sheet.
- Bake until Brie melts, 5 to 6 minutes.
- Divide chopped pecans among prepared phyllo cups. Serve warm.

The Cozy Tea Cart
all about the tea

When Danielle Beaudette decided to expand her retail tea shop in Brookline, New Hampshire, in 2012, she was a little nervous about her plans to add a tearoom. The Cozy Tea Cart had been a successful retailer and wholesaler of tea for more than 10 years.

"For me, it's all about the tea," Danielle explains. "I was afraid running a tearoom would take me away from my love of tea." Then she discovered that one of her customers, Sabine Berke, had trained as a chef in her native Switzerland. "When I told her that I was thinking of opening a café, she offered to be our chef."

As it turned out, the two women had similar ideas about food. Danielle insisted everything had to be made from scratch, and the tearoom had to support local farmers. Sabine replied that was the way people cooked in Switzerland. "Adding Sabine to our staff has worked out phenomenally," Danielle says. "She's an amazing chef."

Having Sabine to hold down the fort at The Cozy Tea Cart has freed Danielle to focus on what she loves most—tea. Years before, Danielle had been among the first graduates of the United States Specialty Tea Institute. Now she travels a great deal, giving lectures. "The more people are educated about tea, the more they will enjoy it," she says.

Danielle also travels to tea countries of origin such as China, India, and Sri Lanka at least once a year. She sources some of her teas directly from the growers there. "I absolutely love what I do," she says.

Tomato Tart

Yield: 8 servings | *Preparation: 45 minutes* | *Bake: 35 to 40 minutes*

2½ pounds ripe tomatoes, cut into thin slices
3 teaspoons sea salt, divided
1½ cups all-purpose flour
¼ cup plus 1 tablespoon yellow cornmeal
4 tablespoons cold salted butter, cut into pieces
1½ cups fresh sweet corn kernels (2 to 4 ears)
2 tablespoons sour cream
1 tablespoon fresh lemon juice
½ cup shredded fontina cheese
2 tablespoons chopped fresh oregano
4 tablespoons thinly sliced fresh basil
¼ teaspoon ground black pepper

• Place tomato slices on layered paper towels, sprinkle with 1 teaspoon salt, and let stand for 15 minutes. Blot excess juice dry with paper towels.
• Meanwhile, in the work bowl of a food processor, combine flour, ¼ cup cornmeal, and 1 teaspoon salt. Pulse twice to mix. Add cold butter, and pulse 5 to 6 times until mixture resembles coarse meal. Transfer mixture to a large bowl, and refrigerate until needed.
• Clean work bowl.
• In work bowl, combine corn kernels, sour cream, and lemon juice. Process until smooth.
• Remove flour mixture from refrigerator. Add corn mixture to cold flour mixture, stirring until a soft dough forms. Knead gently 4 to 5 times, and shape into a ball. Set aside.
• Place a large piece of parchment paper (approximately 16 inches long) on a large cutting board. Sprinkle parchment with remaining 1 tablespoon cornmeal. Transfer dough to prepared parchment paper. Press dough into a 5- to 6-inch circle. Cover with 2 (16-inch) lengths of overlapping plastic wrap. Using a rolling pin, roll covered dough out to a 14- to 15-inch circle. Freeze on cutting board for approximately 10 minutes until dough is firm.
• Preheat oven to 400°.

- Transfer dough on parchment paper to a rimmed baking sheet. Carefully remove plastic wrap.
- In a small bowl, combine cheese and oregano, stirring to blend.
- Remove dough from freezer. Spread cheese mixture onto dough, leaving a 1-inch border. Arrange tomatoes in layers over cheese, sprinkling each layer with remaining 1 teaspoon salt. (If using extra-juicy, farm-fresh tomatoes, it may be necessary to combine 3 tablespoons flour with this salt and sprinkle with a fine-mesh sieve.)
- Fold edges of dough toward center, pressing slightly. (Tomatoes will be only partially covered.)
- Bake until crust is brown, 35 to 40 minutes. Let cool for 10 minutes.
- Top with fresh basil and pepper just before serving.

Make-Ahead Tip: Artichoke Frittata can be baked up to 3 hours in advance and served at room temperature.

Artichoke Frittata

Gluten-free | *Yield: 1 (9-inch) frittata (approximately 8 servings)* | *Preparation: 20 minutes* | *Bake: 23 minutes*

5 large eggs
¾ cup whole milk
1 tablespoon salted butter, melted
1½ teaspoons chopped fresh oregano
½ teaspoon fresh lemon zest
¼ teaspoon ground black pepper
1 (14-ounce) can artichoke hearts, drained, chopped, and squeezed dry
½ cup shredded sharp provolone cheese
Garnish: mascarpone cheese, fresh oregano sprig

• Preheat oven to 375°.
• Spray a shallow 9-inch glass pie plate with cooking spray. Set aside.
• In a medium bowl, combine eggs, milk, melted butter, chopped oregano, lemon zest, and pepper, whisking to blend. Add artichokes and provolone cheese, stirring until incorporated. Pour into prepared pie plate.
• Bake until frittata is set and slightly puffed, approximately 23 minutes. Let cool slightly before removing from pie plate.
• Serve warm or at room temperature.
• Garnish with a swirl of mascarpone cheese and an oregano sprig, if desired.

Creamy Crab-Artichoke Tartlets

Yield: 8 (2½-inch) tartlets | *Preparation: 45 minutes*
Bake: 5 to 7 minutes | *Cool: 30 minutes* | *Cook: 5 minutes*

½ (14.1-ounce) package refrigerated pie dough (1 sheet)
2 tablespoons salted butter
2 tablespoons all-purpose flour
1 cup heavy whipping cream
½ cup whole milk
1 cup lump crabmeat
⅓ cup finely chopped canned artichoke hearts
2 tablespoons diced pimientos
1 tablespoon finely chopped green onion (green tops)
1 tablespoon finely chopped parsley
1 tablespoon dry sherry
½ teaspoon salt
¼ teaspoon ground black pepper
⅛ teaspoon ground nutmeg
Garnish: finely grated Parmesan cheese, ground paprika

• Preheat oven to 450°.
• On a lightly floured surface, unroll pie dough. Using a 2¾-inch round cutter, cut 8 rounds from pie dough.

TARTLET CRUST how-to on page 128

Lightly spray 8 (2½-inch) tartlet pans with cooking spray. Press dough rounds into prepared tartlet pans, trimming excess. Using the large end of a chopstick, press dough into indentations in sides of tartlet pans.
• Place tartlet pans on a rimmed baking sheet. Refrigerate for 30 minutes.
• Prick tartlet dough with a fork to prevent puffing during baking.
• Bake until golden brown, 5 to 7 minutes. Let cool completely. Carefully remove tartlet shells from pans. Set aside in an airtight container at room temperature until ready to fill.
• In a medium nonstick sauté pan, melt butter over medium heat. Add flour, whisking and cooking for 3 minutes until a smooth paste forms. Add cream and milk, whisking until smooth. Add crab, artichokes, pimiento, green onion, parsley, sherry, salt, pepper, and nutmeg, stirring to blend. Cook over low heat until heated through, approximately 5 minutes.
• Divide warm crab mixture among prepared tartlet shells.
• Garnish each with a sprinkle of Parmesan cheese and paprika, if desired.
• Serve immediately.

Make-Ahead Tip: Crab mixture can be made a day in advance and refrigerated in a covered container. Rewarm gently over low heat. Tartlet shells are best made the same day.

Poppyseed Chicken Tartlets

Yield: 20 (2¾-inch) tartlets | *Preparation: 45 minutes*
Bake: 5 to 7 minutes | *Cook: 5 minutes* | *Cool: 30 minutes*

1 (14.1-ounce) package refrigerated pie dough
    (2 sheets)
4 tablespoons salted butter
4 tablespoons all-purpose flour
1½ cups chicken stock
¼ teaspoon ground black pepper
¼ cup sour cream
1 tablespoon finely chopped fresh tarragon
1 tablespoon poppy seeds
1 tablespoon lemon juice
2 cups chopped, cooked chicken
Garnish: finely chopped toasted pecans

• Preheat oven to 450°.
• On a lightly floured surface, unroll pie dough. Using a 2¾-inch round cutter, cut 20 rounds from pie dough. Lightly spray 20 (2¼-inch) tartlet pans with cooking spray. Press dough rounds into prepared tartlet pans, trimming excess. Using the large end of a chopstick, press dough into indentations in sides of tartlet pans.
• Place tartlet pans on a rimmed baking sheet. Refrigerate for 30 minutes.
• Prick tartlet dough with a fork to prevent puffing during baking.
• Bake until golden brown, 5 to 7 minutes. Let cool completely. Carefully remove tartlet shells from pans. Set aside in an airtight container at room temperature until ready to fill.
• In a large nonstick sauté pan, melt butter over medium heat. Add flour, whisking and cooking for 3 minutes until a smooth paste forms. Add stock and pepper, whisking until smooth. Add sour cream, tarragon, poppy seeds, and lemon juice, whisking until incorporated. Add chicken, and cook until heated through.
• Divide warm chicken mixture among prepared tartlet shells. Garnish with chopped pecans, if desired.
• Serve immediately.

Make-Ahead Tip: Chicken mixture can be made a day in advance and refrigerated in an airtight container. Rewarm gently over low heat. Tartlet shells are best made the same day.

Goat Cheese, Date, and Prosciutto Phyllo Cups

Yield: 15 mini tartlets | *Preparation: 25 minutes*

4 ounces goat cheese, at room temperature
4 ounces cream cheese, softened
¼ cup coarsely chopped prosciutto
¼ cup coarsely chopped dates
1 tablespoon heavy whipping cream
2 teaspoons fresh thyme leaves
¼ teaspoon ground black pepper
15 mini phyllo cups
Garnish: fresh thyme sprigs

• In the work bowl of a food processor, combine goat cheese, cream cheese, prosciutto, dates, cream, thyme, and pepper. Pulse until well blended and prosciutto and dates are finely chopped enough to pass through a piping tip.
• Transfer mixture to a piping bag fitted with a large open-star tip (Wilton #1M). To prevent cups from becoming soggy, pipe cheese mixture into phyllo cups just before serving.
• Garnish each with a fresh thyme sprig, if desired.

Make-Ahead Tip: Cheese mixture can be made a day in advance and refrigerated in a covered container until needed. For ease of piping, let soften before using.

TARTLET
CRUST
how-to on
page 128

The Mad Hatter
in a perfect place

A historic home, built in the 1800s, would be the ideal venue for a tearoom. That's what Liz Koch thought when she was planning to open one in 1999. She had in mind the old Woodbury House in Anoka, Minnesota. "It's beautiful," Liz says. "I used to drive by it and think it would be the perfect place for a teahouse." The circa-1857 home was a private residence at the time, however. So Liz settled for a small retail space in the town's original post office, and her tearoom, My Mom's Attic, was born.

Fast-forward to 2013, when Liz and her husband, Tim, wanted to expand the tearoom, now renamed The Mad Hatter. The Woodbury House had passed through several hands since 1999. The city of Anoka now owned it and wanted to ensure that the oldest home in the town would be preserved as a historic site. The Kochs were just two of many locals who submitted a proposal outlining the way they would use the home. In November 2013, the couple got the word—the Woodbury House lease was theirs.

Renovation started that same month. The original Mad Hatter tearoom closed in December 2013, and by Mother's Day 2014, the new one had reopened as a full-service restaurant—offering lunch, dinner, Saturday brunch, and, of course, afternoon tea.

Liz thinks she knows why The Mad Hatter got the city's nod. Their proposal laid out plans to expand the tearoom to a full-service, fine-dining restaurant, which Anoka did not have at the time. Plus, the Mad Hatter had been in business since 1999, and the Kochs had a proven track record.

"Anoka is kind of a Mayberry town," Liz explains. "Your neighbors know you, and you know your neighbors. It's a close-knit community." Being chosen to revive the Woodbury House was a great honor. "It's been so exciting to do this in a community where I raised my kids and have had a business for so many years."

Curried Egg Salad in Puff Pastry Cups

Yield: 24 servings | Preparation: 20 minutes
Refrigerate: 4 hours

6 large hard-boiled eggs, peeled
3 tablespoons mango chutney,
    such as Major Grey's
1 to 3 tablespoons mayonnaise
1 tablespoon Dijon-style mustard
1½ teaspoons curry powder
1 tablespoon chopped fresh chives
¼ teaspoon salt
¼ teaspoon ground black pepper
1 (9.5-ounce) box frozen puff pastry cups
    (24 pastry cups), such as Pepperidge
    Farm, thawed and baked according
    to package directions
Garnish: fresh parsley leaves

• In a large bowl and using a pastry blender, finely chop eggs. Add mango chutney, mayonnaise (to taste and desired consistency), mustard, curry powder, chives, salt, and pepper, stirring well. Refrigerate in an airtight container until cold, approximately 4 hours.
• Using a small levered scoop, divide egg salad among puff pastry cups.
• Garnish each with a parsley leaf, if desired.
• Serve immediately.

Tea Sandwiches & Canapés

TARRAGON-SHRIMP SALAD
FINGER SANDWICHES
(recipe on page 94)

CUCUMBER CANAPÉS
(recipe on page 83)

Make-Ahead Tips
for
Tea Sandwiches

- In general, fillings and spreads for tea sandwiches can be made a day in advance. Refrigerate in a covered container until needed.
- Bread shapes for tea sandwiches can be cut a day in advance and stored in a resealable plastic bag at room temperature.
- Tea sandwiches can be assembled a few hours ahead and refrigerated in a covered container until serving time. Be sure to cover sandwiches with damp paper towels so they don't dry out before serving.
- For even layers when making triple-stack sandwiches, measure filling, and spread equal amounts between bread slices.
- To create clean cuts, wipe knife between each cut.
- When using a cutter, it is easier to make neat cuts if bread is frozen. Let thaw before serving.
- Add any garnishes just before serving.

Creole Egg Salad Tea Sandwiches

Yield: 12 tea sandwiches | *Preparation: 30 minutes*
Refrigerate: 4 hours | *Thaw: 30 minutes*

8 large hard-boiled eggs, peeled
⅓ cup mayonnaise
3 tablespoons Creole mustard, such as Zatarain's
¼ cup finely chopped celery
3 tablespoons dill pickle relish
¼ teaspoon ground black pepper
12 large slices multigrain bread, such as Arnold Multi-Grain, frozen
Garnish: watercress

- In a medium bowl and using a pastry blender, chop eggs into small pieces. Add mayonnaise, mustard, celery, pickle relish, and pepper, stirring to blend. Cover, and refrigerate until cold, approximately 4 hours.
- Using a 3¾-x-2-inch diamond-shaped cutter, cut 24 shapes from frozen bread slices, discarding scraps.
- Divide egg salad evenly among 12 bread diamonds. Top with remaining bread diamonds. Cover with damp paper towels, and let bread thaw completely (approximately 30 minutes) before serving.
- Garnish each tea sandwich with watercress, if desired.

Ham Salad Triple Stacks

Yield: 16 tea sandwiches | *Preparation: 30 minutes*
Thaw: 30 minutes

1 (1.5-pound) center-cut ham steak, prepared according to package instructions and cooled
½ cup mayonnaise
⅓ cup golden raisins
⅓ cup finely chopped celery
2 tablespoons finely chopped fresh chives
1 tablespoon fresh lemon juice
16 slices rye sandwich bread, frozen
8 slices pumpernickel sandwich bread, frozen
Garnish: fresh chives

- In the work bowl of a food processor, process ham until finely chopped.
- In a medium bowl, combine chopped ham, mayonnaise, raisins, celery, chives, and lemon juice, stirring until well blended. Set aside.
- Using a 2-inch hexagonal-shaped cutter, cut 32 shapes from frozen rye bread slices and 16 shapes from frozen pumpernickel bread slices, discarding scraps.
- Spread 1 tablespoon ham salad onto a rye bread shape. Top with a pumpernickel bread shape, and spread another 1 tablespoon ham salad. Top with another rye bread shape to create a triple-stack sandwich. Repeat with remaining bread shapes and ham salad. Cover with damp paper towels, and let bread thaw completely (approximately 30 minutes) before serving.
- Garnish with chives, if desired.

Crab Cake Crostini

Yield: 22 canapés | Preparation: 25 minutes
Refrigerate: 30 minutes | Cook: 2 minutes

1 (8-ounce) container fresh, pasteurized
    lump crabmeat
1 cup panko (Japanese bread crumbs), divided
1 large egg
1 tablespoon minced red bell pepper
1 tablespoon mayonnaise
1 tablespoon fresh lemon juice
1 teaspoon minced shallot
¼ teaspoon salt
⅛ teaspoon ground black pepper
⅓ cup olive oil
1 recipe Lemon-Lime Aïoli (recipe follows)
22 prepared French bread crostini
Garnish: chives, red bell pepper flowers*

• In a medium bowl, combine crabmeat, ¼ cup panko, egg, minced bell pepper, mayonnaise, lemon juice, shallot, salt, and pepper, stirring to blend. Divide crabmeat mixture into 22 equal portions. Shape each portion into a cake, and coat with remaining ¾ cup panko. Place crab cakes on a rimmed baking sheet, and refrigerate for 30 minutes.
• In a large nonstick skillet, heat olive oil over medium-high heat. When oil is hot, cook crab cakes in batches until golden brown, 1 to 2 minutes per side. Drain on paper towels.
• Spoon ¼ teaspoon Lemon-Lime Aïoli onto each crostini, and top with a crab cake. Top each crab cake with another ¼ teaspoon aïoli.
• Garnish each canapé with chives and a bell pepper flower, if desired.
• Serve immediately.

Make-Ahead Tip: Crab cakes can be pan-fried and then refrigerated until needed. To warm, place on a parchment-lined baking sheet, and heat for 5 minutes in a 350° oven.

Lemon-Lime Aïoli

Gluten-free | Yield: ¼ cup | Preparation: 5 minutes

¼ cup mayonnaise
½ teaspoon fresh lime zest
½ teaspoon fresh lemon zest
1 teaspoon fresh lime juice
1 teaspoon fresh lemon juice

• In a small bowl, combine mayonnaise, zests, and juices, whisking to blend. Cover, and refrigerate until needed, up to a day.

Olive-Pecan Finger Sandwiches

Yield: 12 tea sandwiches | Preparation: 20 minutes

1 (8-ounce) package cream cheese, softened
1 tablespoon heavy whipping cream
3 tablespoons finely chopped pimiento-stuffed
    green olives
2 tablespoons finely chopped pitted black olives
¼ cup finely chopped toasted pecans
12 slices very thin whole-wheat sandwich bread,
    such as Pepperidge Farm Very Thin Wheat

• In a medium mixing bowl, combine cream cheese and cream. Beat at medium speed with a mixer until smooth. Add green olives, black olives, and pecans, stirring by hand until incorporated.
• Spread cream cheese mixture onto a bread slice. Top with another bread slice, and spread with cream cheese mixture. Top with a third bread slice to make a triple-stack sandwich. Repeat with remaining bread slices and cream cheese mixture.
• Using a serrated bread knife in a gentle sawing motion, trim and discard crusts from sandwiches. Cut each sandwich into 3 finger sandwiches.
• Serve immediately, or cover with damp paper towels, place in a covered container, and refrigerate for a few hours until serving time.

Make-Ahead Tip: Cream cheese mixture can be made a day in advance and refrigerated in a covered container until needed. Let come to room temperature before using.

*Using a small flower-shaped cutter, cut
shapes from fresh bell pepper sections.

"When tea becomes ritual, it takes its place at the heart of our ability to see greatness in small things."

—Muriel Barbery, *The Elegance of the Hedgehog*

Pickled Egg Canapés

Yield: 24 canapés | *Preparation: 30 minutes*
Cook: 7 minutes | *Refrigerate: 3 days*

6 medium eggs
1 (15-ounce) can sliced beets, drained and juice
    reserved for pickling liquid, beets reserved for
    Apple-Beet Slaw
6 tablespoons white distilled vinegar
2 tablespoons firmly packed light brown sugar
¼ teaspoon whole allspice berries
¼ teaspoon salt
12 slices firm white sandwich bread, such as
    Pepperidge Farm Farmhouse Style White, frozen
2 tablespoons salted butter, softened
1 recipe Apple-Beet Slaw (recipe follows)

• In a medium saucepan, place eggs, and cover with water. Bring to a boil over high heat, and reduce heat so that water boils gently. Cook, uncovered, for exactly 7 minutes. Remove from heat, and transfer eggs to a bowl filled with ice and water. When eggs are completely cooled, crack shells, and carefully peel away shells. Set aside.
• In a small saucepan, combine reserved juice from beets, vinegar, brown sugar, allspice berries, and salt, and bring to a boil over medium-high heat. Reduce heat, and simmer for 5 minutes. Remove from heat, and let liquid cool to room temperature.
• Place eggs in a large, wide-mouth canning jar. (Don't crowd or pack eggs.) Pour cooled pickling liquid over eggs, making sure that eggs are completely submerged and surrounded by liquid. Screw on lid. Refrigerate for 3 days.
• Preheat oven to 350°.
• Using a 2½-inch triangular cutter, cut 24 shapes from frozen bread slices, discarding crusts. Cover with damp paper towels, and let bread thaw slightly (approximately 15 minutes). Place on a rimmed baking sheet. Spread bread triangles lightly with butter.
• Bake until edges are light golden brown, approximately 7 minutes. Let cool completely.
• Remove eggs from pickling liquid, and blot dry on paper towels. Using an egg slicer, cut slices from eggs. Set aside.

• Divide Apple-Beet Slaw among toast triangles. Top each canapé with a pickled egg slice.
• Serve immediately.

Make-Ahead Tip: Plan ahead, and make pickled eggs at least 3 days in advance. Slaw can be made a day in advance. Toast triangles should be made the same day and stored in a resealable plastic bag.

Kitchen Tip: When making hard-boiled eggs, don't use very fresh eggs, as they are more difficult to peel. Keep uncooked eggs in the refrigerator for 1 to 2 weeks to "age" before boiling, or using a straight pin or a thumbtack, gently pierce rounded end of each egg before boiling—or to ensure good results, do both.

Apple-Beet Slaw

Gluten-free | *Yield: 1½ cups*
Preparation: 20 minutes | *Refrigerate: 4 hours*

Beets reserved from Pickled Egg Canapés recipe
    (recipe above), finely chopped
½ cup finely chopped red apple, such as Gala
⅓ cup finely chopped celery
1 tablespoon finely chopped fresh parsley
1 tablespoon finely chopped green onion
    (green parts only)
2 tablespoons red wine vinegar
1 tablespoon olive oil
1 tablespoon Dijon-style mustard
¼ teaspoon sugar
¼ teaspoon salt
⅛ teaspoon ground black pepper

• In a medium bowl, combine beets, apple, celery, parsley, and green onion, stirring to blend. Set aside.
• In a small jar with a screw-top lid, combine vinegar, olive oil, mustard, sugar, salt, and pepper, shaking vigorously until emulsified. Add vinaigrette to beet mixture, tossing to coat. Cover, and refrigerate until cold, approximately 4 hours.

• Trim ends from cucumbers, and cut into 1½-inch sections. Slice each section vertically to yield 54 cucumber slices in all. Set aside.
• In a small bowl, combine mayonnaise, lemon zest, lemon juice, and salt, whisking until blended. Spread ¼ teaspoon mayonnaise mixture onto each bread slice. Top with 3 cucumber slices, overlapping evenly.
• Garnish each canapé with watercress, if desired.

Make-Ahead Tip: Prepare canapés up to 4 hours before serving, cover with damp paper towels, and refrigerate in an airtight container.

Apple, Ham, and Gouda Tea Sandwiches
Yield: 12 tea sandwiches | Preparation: 25 minutes

12 slices rye-pumpernickel-swirl bread, frozen
½ cup mayonnaise
3 tablespoons whole-grain Dijon-style mustard, such as Maille Old Style Whole Grain Dijon Mustard
1 cup baby kale leaves
12 very thin slices smoked ham
12 thin slices Gouda cheese
12 very thin slices green apple
Garnish: additional slices green apple

• Using a 2¼-inch square cutter, cut 24 squares from frozen bread slices, discarding scraps. Cover with damp paper towels, or store in a resealable plastic bag to prevent drying out while preparing other ingredients.
• In a small bowl, combine mayonnaise and mustard, stirring to blend. Set aside.
• Using the same square cutter as for bread, cut 12 squares from cheese slices. Set aside.
• Spread aïoli onto each bread square.
• Using 12 bread squares (aïoli side up) as a base, assemble 12 sandwiches, stacking ingredients in the following order: kale, cheese, ham (ruffled and gathered to fit bread), apple slice, and another bread square (aïoli side down). Cover with damp paper towels, and let bread thaw completely (approximately 30 minutes) before serving.
• Garnish each tea sandwich with a few apple slices, if desired.

Kitchen Tip: Cut apple slices just before assembling and serving. If making sandwiches a few hours in advance, brush apple slices with lemon juice to prevent browning.

Cucumber Canapés
Yield: 18 canapés | Preparation: 35 minutes

9 slices firm white sandwich bread, such as Pepperidge Farm White
2 English cucumbers
¼ cup mayonnaise
½ teaspoon fresh lemon zest
½ teaspoon fresh lemon juice
¼ teaspoon salt
Garnish: watercress

• Using a serrated knife in a gentle sawing motion, trim and discard crusts from bread. Cut each bread slice into 2 (2½-x-1½-inch) pieces. Cover with damp paper towels, or store in a resealable plastic bag to keep from drying out while preparing other ingredients.

The Tea Leaf
mother knows best

Twenty-five years ago when Sally Collura began taking her mom out to tea, she had no idea that tea would someday turn into her vocation. But mothers have a way of recognizing what their children are capable of. So when Sally started saying, "If I had a tearoom, it wouldn't be just a tearoom," Josephine Collura replied, "So why don't you open a tearoom?"

Once Sally had a business plan, she began looking for a retail location. The space she found was a charming mid-1800s storefront right in the heart of Waltham's historic district. "It was only half the space I had wanted in my business plan, just under 1,000 square feet, but I thought it was doable," Sally recalls. "Investment-wise it has turned out to be the best decision."

In remodeling the building, Sally acted as her own general contractor. She took it right down to the studs, installing new wiring, new walls and ceilings, and a new kitchen. "It was a labor of love, and The Tea Leaf really is who I am, in a way."

The result, Sally says, is not just a tearoom. "It's a feast for the eyes." Into the 1,000 square feet of The Tea Leaf, she has packed a seven-table tearoom and a retail shop with one of the best selections of teas in New England. In addition to teas from Harney & Sons, Republic of Tea, and Tea Forté, as well as British brands such as Twinings and Yorkshire Gold, The Tea Leaf also sells Sally's own blends. Both the tearoom and the retail shop have developed quite a following in Waltham.

Josephine passed away in May 2011, but she lived long enough to see The Tea Leaf become a reality. "My mom and I were very close, and I took her everywhere with me. She never discouraged me from doing anything," Sally explains.

Sally's Cucumber–Cream Cheese Tea Sandwiches
Yield: 48 tea sandwiches | Preparation: 25 minutes Refrigerate: 1 hour

½ cup small Spanish olives stuffed with pimiento, drained and 1 tablespoon juice reserved
2 (8-ounce) packages cream cheese, softened
1½ teaspoons dried dill
¼ teaspoon ground black pepper
1 English cucumber
24 slices white sandwich bread

• In the work bowl of a food processor, place olives, and pulse until very finely chopped. Add cream cheese, olive juice, dill, and pepper, and process until a spreadable consistency is achieved. Cover, and refrigerate for 1 hour.
• Using a mandoline, slice cucumber diagonally into very thin slices. Place slices on paper towels. Top with additional paper towels, and pat to remove moisture.
• Spread each bread slice with cream cheese mixture. Arrange cucumber slices evenly on 12 bread slices (cream cheese side up), overlapping cucumber slices. Top with remaining 12 bread slices.
• Using a serrated bread knife in a gentle sawing motion, trim and discard crusts from sandwiches. Cut each sandwich diagonally into 4 triangles.
• Serve immediately, or cover with damp paper towels, place in a covered container, and refrigerate for a few hours until serving time.

Beef au Poivre and Watercress Tea Sandwiches

Yield: 6 to 8 tea sandwiches | Preparation: 25 minutes
Cook: 10 minutes | Bake: 5 minutes | Cool: 30 minutes

1 (6-ounce) beef tenderloin fillet
1 teaspoon whole black peppercorns
1 teaspoon whole green peppercorns
1 teaspoon whole white peppercorns
¼ cup plus 2 teaspoons butter, softened, divided
¼ cup sliced shallot
1 tablespoon plus 1 teaspoon olive oil, divided
¼ teaspoon garlic salt
6 to 8 small Parkerhouse rolls, such as Sister Schubert's
⅓ cup watercress

• Preheat oven to 350°.
• Line a baking sheet with foil. Set aside.
• Remove beef from refrigerator, and let stand at room temperature for 30 minutes before cooking.
• Coarsely chop or grind peppercorns, and combine in a small bowl. Set aside.
• In a sauté pan, heat 2 teaspoons butter over medium-high heat. Add shallot, and reduce heat to low. Cook, stirring occasionally, until shallot is soft and lightly browned. Let cool. Chop finely, and set aside.
• Drizzle beef with 1 tablespoon olive oil. Season with garlic salt. Press peppercorns onto all sides of beef.
• In a small oven-safe sauté pan or a cast-iron skillet, heat remaining 1 teaspoon olive oil over high heat. Add beef, and sear on all sides until browned and lightly charred, approximately 2 minutes per side. Transfer beef to prepared baking sheet.
• Bake for 5 minutes for rare, longer for a greater degree of doneness. (Fillet will feel very springy when pressed with a finger after cooking for a short time; this indicates a rare interior. If meat feels very firm when pressed, it is more well done.) Wrap beef in foil, and let stand for 15 minutes before slicing.
• Using a sharp knife, slice across grain into ¼-inch slices. Set aside.
• In a small bowl, combine cooled shallot and remaining ¼ cup butter, stirring until combined.
• Slice rolls in half horizontally. Spread shallot butter on insides of rolls. Arrange a beef slice over bottom half of each roll (ruffling to fit roll), and tuck in a piece of watercress. Top with remaining halves of rolls (buttered side down).
• Serve immediately.

Make-Ahead Tip: *Beef fillet can be cooked in advance and refrigerated for up to a day. Before serving, heat in a 350° oven just until warm, approximately 5 minutes.*

Tomato, Basil, and Bacon Canapés

Yield: 24 canapés | Preparation: 20 minutes
Thaw: 30 minutes

12 slices firm wheat sandwich bread, frozen
2 tablespoons mayonnaise
24 small leaves fresh basil
24 slices cherry tomato (approximately 8 tomatoes)
2 tablespoons crumbled cooked bacon

• Using a 1½-inch square cutter, cut 24 squares from frozen bread slices, discarding crusts. Cover with damp paper towels, and let bread thaw completely (approximately 30 minutes).
• Spread ¼ teaspoon mayonnaise onto each bread square. Top each with a basil leaf, a tomato slice, and ¼ teaspoon bacon.
• Serve immediately, or cover with slightly damp paper towels to prevent drying out, and refrigerate for up to 30 minutes.

"There are few hours in life more agreeable than the hour dedicated to the ceremony known as afternoon tea."

—Henry James, *The Portrait of a Lady*

Smoked Tuna Tea Sandwiches

Yield: 12 tea sandwiches | Preparation: 30 minutes
Refrigerate: 4 hours | Thaw: 30 minutes

1 (12-ounce) can albacore tuna, drained
2 tablespoons mayonnaise
2 tablespoons finely chopped celery
1 tablespoon chopped green onion
1 tablespoon sour cream
1½ teaspoons finely ground Lapsang Souchong
    dry tea leaves*
1 teaspoon fresh lemon juice
¼ teaspoon Worcestershire sauce
⅛ teaspoon salt
⅛ teaspoon ground black pepper
12 slices light rye bread, frozen
½ cup arugula leaves
12 slices Campari tomato
¾ cup loosely packed alfalfa sprouts
Garnish: arugula leaves, frilled pick

• In a medium bowl, combine tuna, mayonnaise, celery, green onion, sour cream, ground tea, lemon juice, Worcestershire sauce, salt, and pepper, stirring until blended. Transfer mixture to a covered container, and refrigerate until well chilled, approximately 4 hours.
• Using a 2¼-inch round cutter, cut 24 rounds from frozen bread slices, discarding scraps. Cover with damp paper towels, or store in a resealable plastic bag to prevent drying out while preparing other ingredients.
• Using 12 bread rounds as a base, assemble 12 sandwiches, stacking ingredients in the following order: 3 arugula leaves, tuna mixture, 1 tomato slice, sprouts, and another bread round. Cover with damp paper towels, and let bread thaw completely (approximately 30 minutes) before serving.
• Garnish each tea sandwich with an arugula leaf and a frilled pick, if desired.

*Lapsang Souchong is a very smoky Chinese black tea. For a list of fine tea purveyors, see page 132.

CUCUMBER FLOWER
how-to on page 130

Mango Chutney–Cucumber Flower Canapés

Yield: 12 canapés | Preparation: 30 minutes
Thaw: 15 minutes

4 slices firm white sandwich bread, such as
    Pepperidge Farm White, frozen
2 tablespoons mango chutney, such as Major Grey's
1 English cucumber

• Using a 1¾-inch round cutter, cut 12 rounds from frozen bread, discarding crusts. Cover with damp paper towels, and let bread thaw slightly (approximately 15 minutes).
• Spread each bread round very thinly with mango chutney.
• Trim ends from cucumber. Using a mandoline, cut 48 very thin slices from cucumber.
• Fold each cucumber slice into quarters. Place 5 folded slices upright on each bread round, unfolding slightly to resember flower petals.

Kitchen Tip: A mandoline is essential for cutting paper-thin slices of cucumber. For testing purposes, we used a Kyocera mandoline, available at Sur La Table (surlatable.com).

Broccoli Salad Roulades

Yield: 12 to 14 (1-inch) slices | *Preparation: 20 minutes*
Refrigerate: 30 minutes to 2 hours

2 cups finely chopped broccoli florets
¼ cup finely chopped red bell pepper
¼ cup coarsely grated carrot
¼ cup finely crumbled cooked bacon
2 tablespoons finely chopped dried cherries
1 tablespoon finely diced purple onion
1 recipe White Balsamic Dressing (recipe follows)
2 large flour tortillas

• In a medium bowl, combine broccoli, bell pepper, carrot, bacon, cherries, onion, and White Balsamic Dressing, stirring well. Set aside.
• Lay tortillas on a work surface. Divide broccoli salad evenly between tortillas, placing salad in a long row in the center of each. Roll tortillas up firmly into cylinders, enclosing salad.
• Using a serrated knife, cut off ends of each rolled-up tortilla to make a neat cylinder approximately 6 to 7 inches long. Wrap each firmly with plastic wrap, and refrigerate for at least 30 minutes and up to 2 hours.
• Remove plastic wrap, and cut roulades into 1-inch slices.
• Serve immediately.

White Balsamic Dressing

Gluten-free | *Yield: ½ cup*
Preparation: 5 minutes | *Refrigerate: 2 hours*

½ cup mayonnaise
2 tablespoons white balsamic vinegar
1 teaspoon sugar
¼ teaspoon salt
¼ teaspoon ground black pepper

• In a small bowl, combine mayonnaise, vinegar, sugar, salt, and pepper, whisking well. Cover, and refrigerate until cold, at least 2 hours and up to a day.

"Tea! Bless ordinary everyday afternoon tea!"

—Agatha Christie

Pork Crostini with Corn-Avocado Relish

Yield: 24 canapés | *Preparation: 35 minutes*
Bake: 20 minutes | *Cook: 1 to 2 minutes*

2 (9- to 12-ounce) pork tenderloins
1 tablespoon plus 1 teaspoon olive oil, divided
½ teaspoon garlic salt
½ teaspoon chili powder
½ teaspoon smoked paprika
¼ teaspoon ground black pepper
1 recipe Crostini (recipe on page 98) or 24 prepared French bread crostini
1 recipe Corn-Avocado Relish (recipe follows)

• Preheat oven to 350°.
• Line a rimmed baking sheet with foil. Place tenderloins on pan. Drizzle evenly with 1 tablespoon olive oil. Season with garlic salt, chili powder, smoked paprika, and pepper, rubbing spices into pork.
• Bake for 20 minutes. Remove tenderloins from oven, and let rest for 15 minutes. (Pork will be rare.) Cut pork into ½-inch slices.
• In a medium nonstick sauté pan, heat remaining 1 teaspoon olive oil over medium-high heat. Add sliced pork, cooking on both sides until pork is no longer pink and is slightly charred, 1 to 2 minutes. Transfer to a plate, and cover to keep warm.
• Place 1 pork slice on each crostini. Top with Corn-Avocado Relish.
• Serve immediately.

Make-Ahead Tip: *Pork tenderloins can be baked a day in advance. Wrap in foil, and refrigerate until needed. Let pork come to room temperature before continuing with recipe.*

Corn-Avocado Relish

Gluten-free | *Yield: 1 cup* | *Preparation: 10 minutes*

½ cup diced ripe avocado
½ cup cooked fresh yellow corn
2 tablespoons minced red onion
2 tablespoons finely chopped orange bell pepper
2 tablespoons fresh lime juice
1 tablespoon canned minced pickled jalapeño pepper, such as Mt. Olive
1 tablespoon olive oil
¼ teaspoon salt
⅛ teaspoon ground black pepper

• In a medium bowl, combine avocado, corn, onion, bell pepper, lime juice, jalapeño pepper, olive oil, salt, and black pepper, tossing to blend. Use immediately.

Flowery Pimiento Cheese Tea Sandwiches

Yield: 12 tea sandwiches | Preparation: 30 minutes
Thaw: 30 minutes

1 (8-ounce) block extra-sharp Cheddar cheese,
    coarsely shredded
¼ cup diced pimientos
⅓ cup mayonnaise
¼ teaspoon ground black pepper
24 slices whole-wheat bread, such as Pepperidge
    Farm Farmhouse 100% Whole Wheat, frozen

• In a medium bowl, combine cheese and pimientos,
stirring well. Set aside.
• In a small bowl, combine mayonnaise and pepper,
whisking well. Add to cheese mixture, stirring to
incorporate. Set aside.
• Using a 2½-inch flower cutter, cut 24 shapes from
frozen bread slices, discarding scraps. Spread 1 tablespoon cheese mixture each onto 12 bread flowers.
Set aside.
• Using a 1-inch round cutter, cut out centers from
remaining 12 bread flowers, discarding centers. Place
each atop a cheese-covered flower, aligning edges.
Cover with damp paper towels, and let bread thaw
completely (approximately 30 minutes) before serving.

Make-Ahead Tip: *Pimiento cheese mixture can be made*
up to 3 days ahead and stored in an airtight container in
the refrigerator.

Tarragon-Shrimp-Salad Finger Sandwiches

Yield: 12 tea sandwiches | Preparation: 20 minutes
Cook: 5 minutes | Refrigerate: 4 hours

4 cups water
3 slices lemon
2 (4-inch) sprigs fresh tarragon
¾ teaspoon salt, divided
½ teaspoon whole green peppercorns
1 pound medium frozen shrimp, thawed,
    peeled, and deveined
½ cup mayonnaise
1 tablespoon minced fresh tarragon
2 teaspoons fresh lemon juice
2 teaspoons fresh lime juice
1 teaspoon minced celery
1 teaspoon minced shallot
⅛ teaspoon ground black pepper
12 slices very thin white sandwich bread,
    such as Pepperidge Farm Very Thin White
Garnish: fresh tarragon sprigs

• In a medium saucepan, combine water, lemon slices,
tarragon sprigs, ½ teaspoon salt, and peppercorns,
and bring to a boil. When mixture just comes to a boil,
immediately remove saucepan from heat, add shrimp,
and cover. Let stand for 5 minutes. Remove shrimp
from poaching liquid, and place in a bowl filled with
ice. Let cool.
• In a medium bowl, combine mayonnaise, minced tarragon, lemon juice, lime juice, celery, shallot, remaining
¼ teaspoon salt, and pepper, whisking to blend. Set aside.
• Remove shrimp from ice, and blot dry with paper towels.
Chop very finely. Add to mayonnaise mixture, stirring until
combined. Place shrimp mixture in a covered container,
and refrigerate until very cold, approximately 4 hours.
• Spread 2 tablespoons shrimp salad onto a bread
slice. Top with another bread slice, and spread with
another 2 tablespoons shrimp salad. Top with a third
bread slice to make a triple-stack standwich. Repeat
with remaining bread slices and shrimp salad.
• Using a serrated knife in a gentle sawing motion,
cut and discard crusts from all sides of bread. Cut
3 rectangular finger sandwiches from each sandwich.
• Serve immediately, or cover with damp paper towels,
place in a covered container, and refrigerate for a few
hours until serving time.
• Garnish each tea sandwich with a fresh tarragon sprig,
if desired.

Clumzy Clover Tea & Treasures
making a difference

When Sherry Maresca was a little girl and her mother scolded her, she often found solace at her grandmother's house. "Sitting there with a pretty little cup of tea and talking to Grandma always seemed to fix everything," Sherry recalls. That's the atmosphere she wanted to re-create for other women when she opened Clumzy Clover Teas & Treasures in Wasilla, Alaska, in 2014.

After just one year in operation, the tearoom in this small town 40 miles northeast of Anchorage has become a haven for women—a place where they can take off their coats, hats, and scarves and relax. The menu changes daily; Sherry posts it on a wipe board every morning. A cream tea with freshly baked scones and fruit, a special tea that adds tea sandwiches, and a more substantial high tea are always on offer, all served with a delicious pot of tea, of course.

Clumzy Clover offers 30 varieties of tea, and Sherry tries to stick to the basics, such as Earl Grey and Jasmine Silver Needle. She does blend some teas just for her Alaskan clientele—a green tea called Aurora Lights (blended with fireweed, the state flower of Alaska) and another dubbed An Evening in Wasilla (black tea blended with lavender, anise seed, and chamomile).

Grateful customers have written notes to Sherry on the backs of their receipts, saying, "Thank you for my refuge." An older woman once came into the tearoom and asked Sherry to sit down with her so she could share her story. "She told me her mom had passed away when she was very young, and she didn't have many memories of her. Then she said, 'When I sat down at this table and I touched this teacup, I remembered my mom in a fond way.'" Sherry cried.

Running a tearoom is a singular experience, she says. "You don't make a lot of money, but you can make a lot of difference."

Sweet Alaskan Salmon Crostini
Yield: 16 canapés | *Preparation: 15 minutes*
Bake: 10 minutes

2 (8-ounce) cans crushed pineapple, drained
2 teaspoons chopped fresh parsley
1 teaspoon garlic powder
1 teaspoon ground turmeric
¼ teaspoon ground cumin
16 slices cocktail rye bread, toasted
1 (14.75-ounce) can pink Alaskan salmon, drained and flaked
16 slices Swiss cheese
Garnish: smoked paprika, capers, diced pimientos, lemon zest curls

• Preheat oven to 375°.
• In a medium bowl, combine pineapple, parsley, garlic powder, turmeric, and cumin, blending well.
• Spread pineapple mixture onto bread slices. Cover pineapple mixture with flaked salmon, approximately 2 tablespoons per canapé. Trim cheese slices to fit bread slices, and place on top of salmon. Place canapés on a baking stone or a rimmed baking sheet.
• Bake for 10 minutes.
• Garnish each canapé with a sprinkle of paprika and with capers, diced pimientos, and a lemon zest curl, if desired.
• Serve immediately.

Clumzy Clover Teas & Treasures | *290 N. Yenlo Street, Suite 102 • Wasilla, Alaska 99687* | *907-232-1900* | clumzyclover.com

Green Grape and Kiwi Chicken Salad Sandwiches

Yield: 6 tea sandwiches | Preparation: 15 minutes
Refrigerate: 4 hours

2 cups chopped, cooked chicken breast
½ cup green grape halves
½ cup chopped kiwi
¼ cup diced celery
¼ cup slivered almonds, toasted
½ cup mayonnaise
1 tablespoon fresh lemon juice
¼ teaspoon salt
⅛ teaspoon ground black pepper
6 small leaves lettuce
6 small croissants, sliced horizontally

• In a medium bowl, combine chicken, grapes, kiwi, celery, and almonds. Set aside.
• In a small bowl, combine mayonnaise, lemon juice, salt, and pepper, whisking well. Add to chicken mixture, stirring until combined. Cover, and refrigerate until cold, approximately 4 hours.
• Just before serving, place a lettuce leaf in each croissant, and divide chicken salad evenly among croissants.

Shrimp Salad Crostini

Yield: 24 canapés | Preparation: 30 minutes
Cook: 10 minutes | Refrigerate: 4 to 8 hours

4 cups water
¼ cup rice vinegar
1 tablespoon Creole seasoning, such as Tony Chachere's
1 pound small/medium shrimp, peeled and deveined
½ cup mayonnaise
2 teaspoons fresh lemon juice
1½ teaspoons hot pepper sauce
¼ teaspoon salt
¼ teaspoon ground black pepper
3 tablespoons finely chopped celery
1 tablespoon finely minced parsley
1 recipe Crostini (recipe follows) or 24 prepared French bread crostini
Garnish: fresh parsley leaves

• In a medium saucepan, combine water, rice vinegar, and Creole seasoning. Bring to a boil over high heat. When mixture just comes to a boil, immediately remove saucepan from heat, add shrimp, and cover. Let stand for 5 minutes. Remove shrimp from poaching liquid, and place in a bowl filled with ice. Let cool.

• In a small bowl, combine mayonnaise, lemon juice, hot sauce, salt, and pepper, whisking until smooth and creamy. Set aside.
• Finely chop cooled shrimp, and place in a medium bowl. Add celery and parsley, tossing to combine. Add mayonnaise mixture to shrimp mixture, stirring until incorporated. Cover, and refrigerate for at least 4 hours and up to 8 hours.
• No more than 30 minutes before serving, divide shrimp salad among crostini.
• Garnish each canapé with a fresh parsley leaf, if desired.

Crostini

Yield: 24 crostini | Preparation: 5 minutes
Bake: 5 minutes | Cool: 15 minutes

24 (¼-inch-thick) slices French bread
2 tablespoons salted butter, softened

• Preheat oven to 350°.
• Spread butter onto each bread slice. Place slices, butter sides up, on a rimmed baking sheet.
• Bake until crisp and light golden brown, approximately 5 minutes. Let cool completely.
• Store crostini in an airtight container for up to a day.

- Bake until tomatillos are completely soft, approximately 30 minutes. Let cool to room temperature.
- Remove and discard skins from tomatillos, reserving pulp. Press pulp from garlic cloves, discarding skins. Combine garlic pulp with tomatillo pulp, stirring until blended.
- In a medium bowl, combine ½ cup tomatillo mixture, avocado, onion, 1 tablespoon lime juice, cumin, and salt, stirring gently. (Add remaining 1 tablespoon lime juice if a stronger lime flavor is desired.)
- Spoon approximately 1 tablespoon avocado mixture onto each crostini.
- Garnish with red bell pepper strips, if desired.

To caramelize onions, heat 2 teaspoons butter in a sauté pan over low heat. Add ¼ cup chopped onion, and cook, stirring occasionally, until onion is tender and slightly browned, 10 to 15 minutes.

Mini Dill Havarti and Turkey Panini
*Yield: 16 sandwiches | Preparation: 20 minutes
Cook: 6 minutes*

½ cup mayonnaise
1 tablespoon fresh lemon juice
⅛ teaspoon ground black pepper
16 slices sourdough French sandwich bread
16 slices deli roast turkey
16 slices deli dill Havarti cheese
2 tablespoons salted butter, softened
16 slices cherry tomatoes
16 sprigs fresh dill

- In a small bowl, combine mayonnaise, lemon juice, and pepper, whisking well. Cover, and refrigerate aïoli until ready to use.
- Using a 2¼-inch square cutter, cut 32 squares from bread slices.
- Spread each bread square with ½ teaspoon aïoli.
- Trim turkey and cheese slices to fit bread squares, and place between 2 bread slices (aïoli sides to the inside). Spread outside of each bread slice with butter.
- Heat a nonstick griddle over medium-high heat.
- Grill each sandwich, pressing down lightly with a spatula to flatten slightly. Cook until golden brown, approximately 3 minutes per side.
- Top each sandwich with a cherry tomato slice and a dill sprig.
- Serve immediately.

Avocado-Tomatillo Crostini
Yield: 24 canapés | Preparation: 15 minutes

8 tomatillos, outer husks removed
2 cloves garlic, unpeeled
1 tablespoon olive oil
2 cups diced ripe avocado (approximately
    2 avocados)
¼ cup caramelized onion*
1 to 2 tablespoons fresh lime juice
¼ teaspoon ground cumin
¼ teaspoon salt
1 recipe Crostini (recipe on page 98) or 24 prepared
    French bread crostini
Garnish: red bell pepper strips

- Preheat oven to 400°.
- Line a rimmed baking sheet with parchment paper. Set aside.
- In a medium bowl, combine tomatillos, garlic, and olive oil, tossing to coat. Spread in a single layer on prepared baking sheet.

Mini Salmon Croquette Canapés

Yield: 20 canapés | Preparation: 15 minutes
Cook: 6 minutes

1 (14.75-ounce) can pink salmon, drained and
    bones and skin removed
1⅓ cups panko (Japanese bread crumbs), divided
2 large eggs
1 tablespoon fresh lemon juice
1 teaspoon dried dill
¼ teaspoon salt
¼ teaspoon ground black pepper
¼ cup vegetable oil
20 leaves spring-mix lettuces
20 prepared French bread crostini or 1 recipe
    Crostini (recipe on page 98)
1 recipe Citrus Aïoli (recipe follows)
Garnish: fresh dill

• In a medium bowl, combine salmon, ⅓ cup panko,
eggs, lemon juice, dill, salt, and pepper, stirring until
well blended.
• Divide salmon mixture into 20 equal portions. Shape
each portion into a 1½-inch croquette, and coat with
remaining 1 cup panko. Flatten croquettes slightly.
• In a large nonstick sauté pan, heat oil over medium-
high heat. Add croquettes to pan, and cook until golden
brown, 3 to 4 minutes per side (longer if croquettes
have been refrigerated). Drain on paper towels.
• Place a lettuce leaf on each crostini, and top with
a croquette and a dollop of Citrus Aïoli.
• Garnish each canapé with fresh dill, if desired.

Make-Ahead Tip: *Croquettes may be prepared a day
in advance and refrigerated until ready to cook.*

Citrus Aïoli

Gluten-free | Yield: ½ cup | Preparation: 5 minutes

½ cup mayonnaise
½ teaspoon fresh lemon zest
½ teaspoon fresh lime zest
1 teaspoon fresh lemon juice
1 teaspoon fresh lime juice
1 pinch salt

• In a small bowl, combine mayonnaise, zests, juices,
and salt, whisking until combined. Cover, and refrigerate until needed, up to a day.

Buffalo Chicken and Slaw Canapés

Yield: 16 canapés | Preparation: 30 minutes
Thaw: 15 minutes | Cook: 2 minutes

2 tablespoons mayonnaise
2 teaspoons fresh lime juice
¼ teaspoon sugar
⅛ teaspoon salt
⅛ teaspoon ground black pepper
⅓ cup very finely chopped green cabbage
⅓ cup very finely chopped purple cabbage
¼ cup very finely chopped carrot
1 tablespoon very finely chopped green onion
8 slices sourdough sandwich bread, such as
    Pepperidge Farm Farmhouse Sourdough, frozen
2 tablespoons salted butter, softened
16 thin slices deli buffalo chicken
Garnish: green onion slices

• In a large bowl, combine mayonnaise, lime juice,
sugar, salt, and pepper, whisking until blended. Add
cabbages, carrot, and green onion, stirring to combine.
Cover, and refrigerate until needed, up to a day.
• Using a 2¼-inch round cutter, cut 16 rounds from
frozen bread slices, discarding crusts. Cover with damp
paper towels, and let bread thaw slightly (approximately
15 minutes).
• Spread each bread round with softened butter.
• In a large nonstick sauté pan, toast bread rounds over
high heat until crisp and brown, approximately 1 minute
per side, beginning with buttered side. Let cool slightly.
• Arrange a chicken slice on buttered side of each
bread round, ruffling to fit. Top with slaw.
• Garnish each canapé with green onion slices, if desired.
• Serve immediately.

Reuben Canapés

Yield: 24 canapés | Preparation: 30 minutes
Thaw: 15 minutes | Cook: 4 to 6 minutes
Broil: 1 to 2 minutes

12 slices rye bread, frozen
24 thin slices Swiss cheese
½ cup mayonnaise
3 tablespoons ketchup
1 teaspoon Worcestershire sauce
½ teaspoon prepared horseradish
30 very thin slices deli corned beef
1½ cups sauerkraut, well drained
Garnish: corned beef rosettes*

• Preheat broiler.
• Using a 2¼-inch round cutter, cut 24 rounds from
frozen bread slices, discarding crusts. Cover with damp
paper towels, and let bread thaw slightly (approximately
15 minutes).
• Using the same cutter, cut 24 rounds from cheese
slices. Set aside.
• Heat a nonstick sauté pan over medium-high heat.
Place bread rounds in pan, and toast on each side until
golden brown, 2 to 3 minutes. Set aside.
• In a small bowl, combine mayonnaise, ketchup,
Worcestershire sauce, and horseradish, whisking well.
Spread ½ teaspoon mayonnaise mixture onto each
toasted bread round. Arrange a corned beef slice
on each bread round, ruffling to fit. Top each with a
cheese round.
• Place canapés on a broiler pan. Broil just until cheese
melts, 1 to 2 minutes.
• Divide sauerkraut evenly among canapés.
• Garnish each canapé with a corned beef rosette, if
desired.
• Serve immediately.

**Roll 2-x-¼-inch pieces of corned beef into cylinders,
flaring out edges to create rosettes.*

Roasted Vegetable–Cream Cheese Tea Sandwiches

Yield: 18 finger sandwiches | Preparation: 20 minutes
Bake: 30 to 35 minutes

1 cup ¼-inch carrot slices
1 cup ¼-inch parsnip slices
1 cup chopped (1-inch squares) red bell pepper
1 cup chopped (1-inch squares) yellow bell pepper
1 cup ¼-inch sweet onion slices
1 tablespoon olive oil
1 teaspoon herbes de Provence
1 teaspoon salt
¼ teaspoon ground black pepper
1 (8-ounce) package cream cheese, softened
9 slices whole-wheat bread, such as Pepperidge Farm
    Farmhouse Very Thin 100% Whole Wheat

• Preheat oven to 425°.
• Line a baking sheet with foil. Set aside.
• In a large bowl, combine vegetables, olive oil, herbes
de Provence, salt, and black pepper, tossing until well
coated. Spread in a single layer on prepared baking
sheet.
• Bake until vegetables are tender, 30 to 35 minutes.
Let cool slightly. Chop finely.
• In a medium bowl, combine cream cheese and
roasted vegetables, stirring well.
• Spread cream cheese mixture onto a bread slice.
Top with another bread slice, and spread with cream
cheese mixture. Top with a third bread slice to make
a triple-stack sandwich. Repeat with remaining bread
slices and cream cheese mixture.
• Using a serrated bread knife in a gentle sawing
motion, trim and discard crusts from sandwiches.
Cut each sandwich into 6 finger sandwiches.
• Serve immediately, or cover with damp paper towels,
place in a covered container, and refrigerate for a few
hours until serving time.

*Make-Ahead Tip: Cream cheese mixture can be made
a day in advance and refrigerated in a covered container
until needed. Let come to room temperature before using.*

*"It is the personal choices and individual creative touches to
the tiered stand that make teatime such a timeless pleasure."*

—Jane Pettigrew

Gypsy's Tearoom
a compassionate heart

Everyone who owns a tearoom brings their own experiences to the calling. For some, it may be a love of tea or a passion for baking. For Gypsy Fleck of Gypsy's Tearoom in Westminster, Maryland, it's her 30 years of experience as a nurse—the last six working in hospice care—that influence the atmosphere of her tearoom. Gypsy, also known as Jo, feels called to provide a place where her guests can enjoy an hour or two of peace with a cup of tea.

Gypsy opened her business as a retail shop in 1997. After she hosted a Mother's Day Tea and a Christmas Tea in 1998, her customers asked her to expand Gypsy's to include a tearoom. That was 16 years ago, and Gypsy's Tearoom has been a community favorite ever since.

"The most rewarding side of owning a tearoom is interacting with the guests and teaching them about tea," Gypsy explains. "I love sharing that knowledge and suggesting teas for them to try." The tearoom offers an extensive line of teas, from Harney & Sons to Taylors of Harrogate, and they blend their own teas as well. "I especially like it when men come into the tearoom. That's a good sign to me," she says. "I think men are afraid they're not going to get enough to eat at a tearoom, but they never go away hungry here. Our food is very filling."

Gypsy's Tearoom is located in the 18th-century William Winchester House, which Gypsy leases from Target Community Services, a Carroll County agency that works to enhance the lives of adults with disabilities. "They train adults with disabilities for jobs, and we have consistently provided that opportunity for them," she explains. It's a way of giving back to the community that has supported her business for 18 years.

Apple, Walnut, and Cranberry Crostini

Yield: 36 canapés | Preparation: 20 minutes
Bake: 7 to 9 minutes

1 (11-ounce) French baguette (approximately 18 inches long)
1 (8-ounce) package cream cheese, softened
4 ounces goat cheese, at room temperature
3 small Granny Smith apples, cored and thinly sliced
¼ cup honey
¼ cup dried cranberries, finely chopped
¼ cup finely chopped walnuts

• Preheat oven to 350°.
• Line 2 rimmed baking sheets with parchment paper. Set aside.
• Using a serrated bread knife, cut ½-inch slices from baguette. Place on prepared baking sheets.
• Bake until crisp and lightly brown, 7 to 9 minutes. Let cool.
• In the work bowl of a food processor, combine cream cheese and goat cheese, pulsing until smooth. Spread generously onto toasted baguette slices (crostini).
• Arrange 2 apple slices on each crostini. Drizzle apples with honey. Sprinkle with cranberries and walnuts.
• Serve immediately.

Make-Ahead Tip: *Baguette slices can be toasted earlier in the day, cooled, and stored in an airtight container at room temperature until needed.*

Italian BLT Tea Sandwiches

Yield: 12 tea sandwiches | Preparation: 45 minutes
Cook: 5 minutes | Thaw: 30 minutes

6 slices soft Italian sandwich bread, such as Arnold, frozen
1 (24-ounce) jar whole roasted red peppers
12 slices pancetta*
1 teaspoon olive oil
1 eggplant†, peeled and cut into 12 (¼-inch) slices
⅛ teaspoon garlic salt
⅛ teaspoon ground black pepper
¼ cup water
1 recipe Lemon-Oregano Aïoli (recipe follows)
12 leaves green leaf lettuce
12 slices Campari tomato
Garnish: fresh oregano sprigs, frilled picks

• Using a 2½-inch round cutter, cut 24 rounds from frozen bread slices, discarding scraps. Cover with damp paper towels, or store in a resealable plastic bag to keep from drying out while preparing other ingredients.
• Using the same cutter, cut 12 rounds from roasted red peppers. Drain on paper towels, and set aside.
• In a large nonstick sauté pan, cook pancetta over medium-high heat until crisp, 3 to 4 minutes, turning halfway through cooking. Drain on paper towels, and set aside.
• In the same pan, heat olive oil over medium-high heat.
• Sprinkle eggplant slices with garlic salt and pepper. Sear in hot pan for 1 to 2 minutes, add ¼ cup water, and cover pan with lid. Reduce heat to medium-low. Cook for 3 to 4 minutes, turning halfway through cooking, until eggplant is tender when pierced with a fork. Set eggplant aside.
• Spread Lemon-Oregano Aïoli onto each bread round. Using 12 bread rounds (aïoli sides up) as a base, assemble 12 sandwiches, stacking ingredients in the following order: lettuce, tomato, eggplant, red pepper round, pancetta, and another bread round (aïoli side down). Cover with damp paper towels, and let bread thaw completely (approximately 30 minutes) before serving.
• Garnish each tea sandwich with an oregano sprig and a frilled pick, if desired.

Lemon-Oregano Aïoli

Gluten-free | Yield: ½ cup | Preparation: 5 minutes

½ cup mayonnaise
1 teaspoon minced fresh oregano
½ teaspoon fresh lemon zest
⅛ teaspoon salt
⅛ teaspoon ground black pepper

• In a small bowl, combine mayonnaise, oregano, lemon zest, salt, and pepper, stirring to blend. Cover, and refrigerate until needed, up to 2 days.

Caper-Celery Egg Salad Tea Sandwiches

Yield: 12 tea sandwiches | Preparation: 30 minutes
Refrigerate: 4 hours | Thaw: 30 minutes

6 large hard-boiled eggs, peeled
3 tablespoons mayonnaise
2 tablespoons whole-grain Dijon-style mustard, such as Maille Old Style Whole Grain Dijon Mustard
2 tablespoons finely chopped celery
1 tablespoon chopped capers
¼ teaspoon ground black pepper
12 slices seedless rye bread, frozen
Garnish: whole capers, baby arugula leaves

• In a medium bowl and using a pastry blender, chop eggs into small pieces. Add mayonnaise, mustard, celery, capers, and pepper, stirring until blended. Cover, and refrigerate until cold, approximately 4 hours.
• Using a 1¾-inch round cutter, cut 24 rounds from frozen bread slices, discarding scraps.
• Divide egg salad evenly among 12 bread rounds. Top with remaining bread rounds. Cover with damp paper towels, and let bread thaw completely (approximately 30 minutes) before serving.
• Garnish each tea sandwich with capers and baby arugula, if desired.

*Pancetta is an Italian bacon that is
cut in round slices and can be found
in the deli of most grocery stores.

†Choose an eggplant approximately
2½ inches in diameter.

Avocado-Egg Salad Canapés

Yield: 48 canapés | Preparation: 30 minutes
Thaw: 15 minutes | Bake: 10 minutes | Cool: 30 minutes

8 hard-boiled eggs, peeled
⅓ cup mayonnaise
3 tablespoons Dijon-style mustard
3 tablespoons finely chopped fresh dill
¼ teaspoon salt
9 slices pumpernickel sandwich bread, frozen
3 avocados
1 whole lemon, cut into quarters
Garnish: fresh dill sprigs

• In a medium bowl and using a pastry blender, chop eggs into small pieces. Add mayonnaise, mustard, dill, and salt, stirring to blend. Cover, and refrigerate until cold, approximately 4 hours.
• Preheat oven to 350°.
• Line a rimmed baking sheet with parchment paper. Set aside.
• Using a 1½-inch scalloped-edge round cutter, cut 48 rounds from bread slices, discarding scraps. Place bread in a single layer on prepared baking sheet. Cover with damp paper towels, and let bread thaw slightly (approximately 15 minutes) before toasting.
• Remove paper towels, and bake for 10 minutes. Let cool completely, and store in a resealable plastic bag until needed.
• Peel whole avocadoes, and cut into thin vertical slices. Squeeze lemon juice over slices to prevent browning. Using the same cutter as for bread, cut 48 rounds from avocado slices.
• Place an avocado slice on top of each toasted bread round. Using a levered 2-teaspoon scoop, place egg salad on top of avocado rounds.
• Garnish with dill sprigs, if desired.
• Serve immediately, or refrigerate, lightly covered, for up to 30 minutes before serving.

Make-Ahead Tip: *Bread rounds can be made earlier in the day and stored in an airtight container at room temperature until needed.*

Herb and Flower Canapés

Yield: 16 canapés | Preparation: 30 minutes
Thaw: 15 minutes

4 slices pumpernickel bread, frozen
4 ounces cream cheese, softened
1 tablespoon fresh lemon juice
⅛ teaspoon salt
Garnish: fresh herbs (such as chives, dill, rosemary, and thyme), edible flowers (such as rosemary and lavender)

• Using a 1½-inch hexagonal cutter, cut 16 shapes from frozen bread slices, discarding crusts. Cover with damp paper towels, and let bread thaw slightly (approximately 15 minutes).
• In a small bowl, combine cream cheese, lemon juice, and salt, stirring until blended. Transfer cream cheese mixture to a piping bag fitted with small round tip.* Pipe a small button of cream cheese onto each bread shape. Using a small offset spatula, smooth cream cheese surface.
• Arrange herbs and flowers on cream cheese layer.
• Serve immediately, or cover with slightly damp paper towels to prevent drying out, and refrigerate for 1 to 2 hours.

*As an alternative, use a resealable bag with the corner snipped off.

Lemon-Oregano Vinaigrette
Gluten-free | *Yield: ½ cup* | *Preparation: 40 minutes*

¼ cup extra-virgin olive oil
¼ cup fresh lemon juice
2 teaspoons finely chopped fresh oregano leaves
1 teaspoon finely chopped shallot
½ teaspoon Dijon-style mustard
½ teaspoon sugar
¼ teaspoon salt
⅛ teaspoon ground black pepper

• In a small jar with a screw-top lid, combine olive oil, lemon juice, oregano, shallot, mustard, sugar, salt, and pepper. Shake vigorously until emulsified. Let vinaigrette stand at room temperature for 30 minutes to allow flavor to develop.
• Use immediately, or cover, and refrigerate until needed, up to 2 days.

Kitchen Tip: *Dried oregano can be substituted for fresh oregano leaves, but decrease the amount by one-half, as the flavor of dried herbs is more intense than that of fresh herbs.*

Vegan Veggie Roulades
Yield: 21 (1-inch) slices | *Preparation: 20 minutes*

¾ cup hummus
3 (9-x-7-inch) flatbreads, such as Joseph's Multi-grain Flatbread
1 cup baby kale leaves
⅓ cup very thinly sliced radishes
⅓ cup very thinly sliced yellow squash
⅓ cup orange bell pepper strips
3 tablespoons golden raisins
3 tablespoons toasted sesame seeds
1 recipe Lemon-Oregano Vinaigrette (recipe follows)

• Spread ¼ cup hummus on each flatbread. Arrange kale on top of hummus in an even layer. Top with radishes, squash, and bell pepper strips. Sprinkle raisins and sesame seeds on top. Drizzle lightly with Lemon-Oregano Vinaigrette.
• Starting from short end of flatbreads, roll up each one firmly, encasing ingredients. Using a serrated bread knife, cut into 1-inch slices.

Make-Ahead Tip: *Roulades can be made a couple of hours in advance, wrapped securely in plastic wrap, and refrigerated until needed. Slice just before serving.*

Fig Diamonds
Yield: 6 tea sandwiches | *Preparation: 20 minutes*
Thaw: 30 minutes

1 (8-ounce) package cream cheese, softened
⅓ cup finely chopped toasted walnuts
¼ cup finely chopped dried figs
1 teaspoon fresh thyme leaves
⅛ teaspoon ground black pepper
12 slices firm white sandwich bread, such as Pepperidge Farm White, frozen
Garnish: fresh thyme sprigs

• In a medium bowl, combine cream cheese, walnuts, figs, thyme leaves, and pepper, stirring to blend. Spread mixture in a thick, even layer onto 6 frozen bread slices. Set aside.
• Using a 3-x-2-inch diamond-shaped cutter, cut shapes from remaining 6 frozen bread slices, discarding scraps. Set aside.
• Using the same cutter, cut 6 shapes from cream cheese–topped bread slices, discarding scraps. Top each with a plain bread diamond. Cover with damp paper towels, and let bread thaw completely (approximately 30 minutes) before serving.
• Garnish each tea sandwich with a thyme sprig, if desired.

Dilly Roast Beef Tea Sandwiches

Yield: 12 tea sandwiches | Preparation: 25 minutes
Thaw: 30 minutes

½ cup mayonnaise
2 tablespoons finely chopped fresh dill
2 tablespoons finely chopped fresh chives
2 tablespoons finely chopped fresh basil
1 tablespoon red wine vinegar
⅛ teaspoon salt
⅛ teaspoon ground black pepper
24 slices white sandwich bread, frozen
12 very thin slices deli-style roast beef
12 sprigs fresh dill
Garnish: additional fresh dill sprigs

• In a small bowl, combine mayonnaise, dill, chives, basil, vinegar, salt, and pepper. Cover, and refrigerate aïoli until ready to use.
• Using a 2½-inch triangular cutter, cut 24 shapes from frozen bread slices.
• Spread ½ teaspoon aïoli onto each bread triangle. Set aside.
• Fold roast beef slices in half, then in half again to create triangles. Arrange roast beef on top of 12 bread triangles (aïoli sides up). Tuck a dill sprig into center of roast beef. Top each sandwich with another bread triangle (aïoli side down). Cover with damp paper towels, and let bread thaw completely (approximately 30 minutes) before serving.
• Garnish each tea sandwich with a fresh dill sprig, if desired.

Kitchen Tip: To keep fresh dill from wilting, soak in ice water for 10 minutes.

Roast Beef Finger Sandwiches with Smoked Paprika–Lime Aïoli

Yield: 9 tea sandwiches | Preparation: 30 minutes

6 slices potato bread, such as Pepperidge Farm
    Farmhouse Style
1 recipe Smoked Paprika–Lime Aïoli (recipe follows)
½ cup baby arugula leaves
27 thin slices Campari tomato
9 ultrathin slices roast beef, such as Hillshire Farm
Garnish: baby arugula leaves

• Using a serrated bread knife in a gentle sawing motion, cut 3 even rectangles from each bread slice, trimming and discarding crusts. Store in a resealable plastic bag, or cover with damp paper towels to prevent drying out.

• Spread ½ teaspoon aïoli onto each bread rectangle. Using 9 bread rectangles (aïoli sides up) as a base, assemble sandwiches, stacking ingredients in the following order: arugula, 3 tomato slices (shingled to fit), roast beef slice (folded in half and gathered to ruffle), and another bread rectangle (aïoli side down).
• Garnish each tea sandwich with an arugula leaf, if desired.

Smoked Paprika–Lime Aïoli
Gluten-free | Yield: ½ cup | Preparation: 10 minutes

½ cup mayonnaise
1 tablespoon finely chopped cilantro
1 teaspoon fresh lime zest
1 teaspoon fresh lime juice
1 teaspoon smoked paprika
½ teaspoon ground cumin

• In a small bowl, combine mayonnaise, cilantro, lime zest, lime juice, paprika, and cumin, stirring to blend. Cover, and refrigerate until needed, up to 2 days

Sisters Tea Parlor & Boutique
connecting women

Moms often put their dreams on hold to raise their children, says Lori Crowe of Sisters Tea Parlor & Boutique in Buckner, Kentucky. But in 2007, Lori's own mom suggested a way to make her daughter's dreams come true.

In 2002, Connie Young had opened Sisters Gift Shop, a boutique that celebrated women, in this small town approximately 20 minutes northeast of Louisville. After five years, she thought the shop needed a little something more. She called her daughter Lori and said, "I think we need to add a tearoom."

"My heart just sang," Lori recalls. "It was perfect timing." The youngest of Lori's three sons had just started to school, and she had the time to devote to the tearoom. Connie moved her business to a new location and renamed it Sisters Tea Parlor & Boutique.

They served their first tea Mother's Day weekend 2007. "It has been an interesting journey filled with a lot of laughter, but also a lot of tears," Lori says. There were times when the women thought they just might have to close the doors.

Lori and Connie had expanded into more retail space next door, adding two dining rooms and a larger kitchen, when the 2008 recession hit. "I thought we should wait, but Mom decided we should take the space," Lori recalls. "That's when I learned that when you make a decision based on fear, more than likely you're going to make the wrong one." Having the additional dining rooms for private parties and the larger kitchen for catering jobs helped the business survive those lean times.

There's a tie that binds women together, Connie says. Every woman has a sister, and every woman is a sister. "That's really been a powerful part of our vision—connecting women," Lori points out. "We say, 'Connect with your grandmother; connect with your granddaughter. Connect with a friend that you haven't seen in 20 years. Connect at the tea table.'"

Sisters Tea Parlor's Chicken Salad Tea Sandwiches

Yield: 18 tea sandwiches | *Preparation: 30 minutes*
Bake: 15 minutes | *Cool: 30 minutes*
Refrigerate: 2 to 4 hours

2 pounds boneless skinless chicken breasts, cleaned and trimmed
¼ cup vegetable oil
1 teaspoon salt, divided
¾ teaspoon ground black pepper, divided
1 (8-ounce) package cream cheese, softened
1 cup heavy whipping cream
1 teaspoon onion powder
1 teaspoon fresh lemon juice
½ teaspoon sugar
1½ cups finely chopped celery
½ cup finely chopped fresh parsley
12 slices multigrain bread, such as Arnold Multi-Grain

• Preheat oven to 400°.
• In a 13-x-9-inch baking dish, toss chicken breasts in oil. Season with ½ teaspoon salt and ¼ teaspoon pepper.
• Bake chicken until browned and cooked through, approximately 15 minutes. Wrap dish tightly in aluminum foil, and let stand for 15 minutes. (Steam will help chicken stay moist and tender.)
• Remove foil from pan, and let chicken cool enough to handle. Finely chop chicken, and set aside.
• In a medium bowl, combine cream cheese, cream, onion powder, lemon juice, sugar, remaining ½ teaspoon salt, and remaining ½ teaspoon pepper, stirring until well blended. Add chicken, celery, and parsley, stirring until well combined. For best flavor, cover, and refrigerate for 2 to 4 hours.

• Spread ½ cup chicken salad onto 6 slices bread. Top with remaining 6 bread slices.
• Using a serrated bread knife in a gentle sawing motion, trim and discard crusts from sandwiches.

Cut each sandwich into 3 finger sandwiches.
• Serve immediately, or cover with damp paper towels, place in a covered container, and refrigerate for a few hours until serving time.

Bacon, Mushroom, and Caramelized Onion Tea Sandwiches

Yield: 12 tea sandwiches | Preparation: 30 minutes
Bake: 20 minutes | Cook: 10 minutes
Cool: 20 minutes | Thaw: 30 minutes

1 cup sliced white button mushrooms
1 teaspoon olive oil
⅜ teaspoon salt, divided
¼ teaspoon ground black pepper, divided
1 tablespoon salted butter
1 cup sliced sweet onion
1 (8-ounce) package cream cheese, softened
1 tablespoon heavy whipping cream
¼ cup finely chopped cooked bacon
1 teaspoon fresh thyme leaves
6 large slices firm whole-wheat bread such as
    Pepperidge Farm Farmhouse Style, frozen
Garnish: fresh thyme sprigs

• Preheat oven to 350°.
• Line a rimmed baking sheet with parchment paper.
• In a small bowl, toss mushrooms with olive oil,
⅛ teaspoon salt, and ⅛ teaspoon pepper to coat.
Spread in a single layer on prepared pan.
• Bake until mushrooms are tender and release their
juices, approximately 20 minutes. Let cool completely.
Finely chop, and set aside.
• In a small nonstick sauté pan, melt butter over
medium-high heat. Add onion, and reduce heat to
medium-low, cooking and stirring occasionally until
onion is tender and lightly caramelized, approximately
10 minutes. Let cool completely. Finely chop, and set
aside.
• In a medium mixing bowl, combine cream cheese,
cream, remaining ¼ teaspoon salt, and remaining
⅛ teaspoon pepper. Beat at medium-high speed with
a mixer until well blended. Add roasted mushrooms,
caramelized onions, bacon, and thyme leaves, stirring
by hand to incorporate.
• Spread a thick layer of mushroom mixture onto
3 frozen bread slices. Top each with another frozen
bread slice.
• Using a 2-inch scalloped-edge round cutter, cut
4 tea sandwiches from each whole sandwich, discarding scraps. Cover with damp paper towels, and let
bread thaw completely (approximately 30 minutes)
before serving.
• Garnish with a fresh thyme sprig, if desired.

Nutty Carrot, Pineapple, and Ginger Tea Sandwiches

Yield: 9 tea sandwiches | Preparation: 25 minutes

1 (8-ounce) package cream cheese, softened
½ teaspoon freshly grated ginger root
½ cup grated carrot (medium grate)
½ cup canned crushed pineapple, well drained
¼ cup chopped, roasted, salted macadamia nuts
9 slices very thin wheat bread, such as Pepperidge
    Farm Very Thin 100% Whole Wheat
Garnish: carrot strips

• In a medium bowl, combine cream cheese, ginger,
carrot, pineapple, and macadamia nuts, stirring until
well blended.
• Spread cream cheese mixture onto a bread slice.
Top with another bread slice, and spread with cream
cheese mixture. Top with a third bread slice to make
a triple-stack sandwich. Repeat with remaining bread
slices and cream cheese mixture.
• Using a serrated bread knife in a gentle sawing
motion, trim and discard crusts from sandwiches.
Cut each sandwich into 3 finger sandwiches.
• Serve immediately, or cover with damp paper towels,
place in a covered container, and refrigerate for a few
hours until serving time.
• Garnish with a carrot strip, if desired.

*Make-Ahead Tip: Cream cheese mixture can be made
a day in advance and refrigerated in a covered container
until needed. Let come to room temperature before using.*

"*A man's social rank is
determined by the
amount of bread he eats
in a sandwich.*"

—F. Scott Fitzgerald

Cilantro-Lime Aïoli
Gluten-free | *Yield: ⅓ cup* | *Preparation: 5 minutes*

⅓ cup mayonnaise
3 tablespoons finely chopped fresh cilantro
1 tablespoon fresh lime zest
1 teaspoon fresh lime juice
⅛ teaspoon salt
⅛ teaspoon pepper

• In a small bowl, combine mayonnaise, cilantro, lime zest, lime juice, salt, and pepper, stirring to blend. Cover, and refrigerate until needed, up to a day.

Gouda-Goat-Pimiento-Cheese Canapés
Yield: 24 canapés | *Preparation: 20 minutes*

1½ cups whole roasted red peppers
8 ounces Gouda cheese, finely shredded
4 ounces goat cheese, at room temperature
¼ cup mayonnaise
½ teaspoon Worcestershire sauce
¼ teaspoon ground black pepper
¼ teaspoon hot pepper sauce, such as Tabasco
24 petits toasts, such as Trois Petits Cochons
    (Three Little Pigs)
Garnish: parsley leaves

• Using a 1-inch linzer-type flower cutter, cut 24 shapes from whole roasted red peppers. Set aside.
• Chop and reserve 3 tablespoons red pepper scraps.
• In a medium bowl, combine Gouda cheese, goat cheese, mayonnaise, chopped red peppers, Worcestershire sauce, black pepper, and hot sauce, stirring to blend. Spread pimiento cheese onto toasts. Top each with a pepper flower.
• Garnish each canapé with a parsley leaf, if desired.

Make-Ahead Tip: Pepper cutouts can be made a day in advance, covered with liquid from roasted red pepper jar, and refrigerated in a covered container. Blot dry on paper towels just before using.

Cucumber-Pear Canapés
Yield: 12 canapés | *Preparation: 35 minutes*

1 English cucumber
3 ripe Bosc pears
1 lime, cut in half
12 large round crackers, such as Breton
    Original Crackers
1 recipe Cilantro-Lime Aïoli (recipe follows)
Garnish: fresh cilantro sprigs

• Trim ends from cucumber. Using a mandoline, cut 36 very thin slices from cucumber. Set aside.
• Using a paring knife, cut 36 very thin slices from pear. Squeeze lime juice over pear slices to prevent browning. Blot dry.
• Spread 1 teaspoon Cilantro-Lime Aïoli onto each cracker. Top with 3 cucumber slices in an overlapping circle. Fan 3 pear slices on top of cucumbers.
• Garnish each canapé with a cilantro sprig, if desired.
• Serve immediately.

Smoked Salmon Salad Canapés

Yield: 8 canapés | Preparation: 20 minutes
Refrigerate: 4 hours

2 (3.75-ounce) cans smoked salmon fillets in oil,
    such as Bumble Bee, drained
2 tablespoons mayonnaise
2 tablespoons finely chopped celery
1 tablespoon finely chopped green onion
    (green parts only)
1 tablespoon fresh lemon juice
2 teaspoons creamy horseradish
⅛ teaspoon ground black pepper
8 rectangular crackers (mini croccantini),
    such as La Panzanella
Garnish: celery leaves, lemon zest curls

• In a medium bowl, flake salmon with a fork. Add mayonnaise, celery, green onion, lemon juice, horseradish, and pepper, stirring to blend. Cover, and refrigerate until cold, approximately 4 hours.
• Spread approximately 2 tablespoons salmon salad onto each cracker.
• Garnish each canapé with a celery leaf and a lemon curl, if desired.

Kitchen Tip: Make lemon curls before juicing lemons! Use a Microplane Ultimate Citrus Tool to create long strips of lemon peel. Wrap strips around a straw to curl. Snip curls to desired lengths.

CHECKER-BOARD
how-to on page 129

Checkerboard Herbed Butter Tea Sandwiches

Yield: 10 to 12 tea sandwiches
Preparation: 30 minutes | Refrigerate: 2 hours

8 tablespoons salted butter, at room temperature
1 tablespoon red wine vinegar
1 tablespoon finely chopped fresh dill
1 tablespoon finely chopped fresh chives
2 teaspoons dried dill
4 slices pumpernickel bread
3 slices seedless rye bread

• In a small bowl, combine butter, vinegar, fresh dill, chives, and dried dill, stirring until well blended. Set aside.
• Using a serrated bread knife in a gentle sawing motion, cut 10 (4-x-1-inch) rectangles from pumpernickel bread slices and 8 from rye bread slices, discarding scraps.

• On a work surface, arrange 3 bread rectangles, long sides together, alternating pumpernickel and rye. Spread a thick even layer of herbed butter onto bread layer, holding rectangles together with fingers. Place 3 more bread rectangles on top, alternating rye and pumpernickel. Spread another thick even layer of herbed butter onto bread layer. Place 3 more bread rectangles on top, alternating pumpernickel and rye. Repeat with remaining bread rectangles and butter. Wrap sandwiches in damp paper towels and plastic wrap, and refrigerate until set, approximately 2 hours.
• Just before serving, unwrap sandwiches. Using a serrated bread knife in a gentle sawing motion, trim and discard uneven ends from sandwiches. Cut each sandwich crossways into ½-inch slices.

Kitchen Tip: We used both fresh and dried dill in these sandwiches to impart a fresh, intense flavor. To chop herbs finely, use kitchen scissors.

Sun-Dried Tomato Aïoli

Gluten-free | *Yield: ½ cup* | *Preparation: 5 minutes*

2 tablespoons minced sun-dried tomato
1 cup boiling water
½ cup mayonnaise
1 teaspoon fresh lemon juice
¼ cup finely grated Parmesan cheese
1 teaspoon chopped fresh thyme
1 teaspoon chopped fresh oregano
¼ teaspoon salt
¼ teaspoon ground black pepper

• In a small bowl, combine sun-dried tomato and boiling water. Let stand for 1 minute to rehydrate. Drain and discard water.
• In another small bowl, combine sun-dried tomato, mayonnaise, lemon juice, Parmesan cheese, thyme, oregano, salt, and pepper, whisking well. Cover, and refrigerate until needed, up to 2 days.

Pickled Okra Roulades

Gluten-free variation | *Yield: 12 to 14 (1-inch) slices*
Preparation: 20 minutes

1 (24-ounce) jar mild pickled okra spears
½ cup spreadable cream cheese, divided
2 (9-inch) sun-dried-tomato flour tortillas*
6 to 8 thin slices deli smoked turkey breast

• Cut stem ends and tips from okra spears. Blot okra dry with paper towels. Set aside.
• Spread 2 tablespoons cream cheese over each tortilla. Place 3 or 4 turkey slices over cream cheese layer on each tortilla. Spread remaining 2 tablespoons cream cheese over turkey layer of each tortilla.
• Starting at end of tortilla closest to you, place a row of 3 okra spears. Make another row of okra spears next to the first row. Place a third row of okra spears on top of first 2 rows. Roll up tortilla away from you, pressing firmly to keep okra spears together. End with seam side down.
• Using a serrated knife, cut off ends of each rolled-up tortilla to make a neat cylinder approximately 6 to 7 inches long. Cut cylinders into 1-inch slices.

To make a gluten-free version, replace flour tortillas with gluten-free garden vegetable–flavored wraps, such as Toufayan Bakeries.

Make-Ahead Tip: *Roulades can be made a couple of hours in advance, wrapped securely in plastic wrap, and refrigerated until needed. Cut into slices just before serving.*

Summertime Ham Sandwiches

Yield: 8 sandwiches | *Preparation: 20 minutes*

8 ciabatta rolls, such as Alexia, baked according
   to package directions and cooled
1 recipe Sun-Dried Tomato Aïoli (recipe follows)
24 leaves spring-mix lettuces
8 slices deli ham
Garnish: decorative wooden picks

• Slice rolls in half horizontally. Spread Sun-Dried Tomato Aïoli evenly inside rolls. Arrange 3 lettuce leaves on bottom half of each roll. Arrange ham on top of lettuce leaves (ruffling to fit roll). Top with remaining halves of rolls (aïoli side down).
• Garnish each sandwich with a decorative pick, if desired.
• Serve immediately.

Beef and Cheddar
Triple-Stack Sandwiches

Yield: 8 tea sandwiches | Preparation: 45 minutes
Cook: 8 to10 minutes | Thaw: 30 minutes

2 (6-ounce) beef tenderloin fillets
1 tablespoon olive oil, divided
¼ teaspoon garlic salt
¼ teaspoon ground black pepper
¼ teaspoon ground half-sharp paprika*
1 teaspoon butter, cut in half
16 slices sourdough sandwich bread,
   such as Pepperidge Farm Farmhouse
   Style Sourdough Bread, frozen
8 slices hearty wheat sandwich bread,
   such as Pepperidge Farm Farmhouse
   Style Wheat, frozen
8 slices sharp Cheddar cheese
1 recipe Horseradish Aïoli (recipe follows)
½ cup baby arugula leaves
24 slices Campari tomatoes
Garnish: decorative picks

- Preheat oven to 350°.
- Line a rimmed baking sheet with foil. Set aside.
- Rub each fillet with 1 teaspoon olive oil. Evenly season on all sides with garlic salt, pepper, and paprika, rubbing spices into filets. Let fillets sit at room temperature for 30 minutes.
- In a nonstick sauté pan, heat remaining 1 teaspoon olive oil over medium-high heat. Add meat to pan, and sear fillets on all sides until browned, 2 to 3 minutes per side. Transfer fillets to prepared baking sheet.
- Bake fillets until desired degree of doneness is reached[†], 5 to 7 minutes for rare. Add more baking time for well done.
- When fillets are cooked, top each piece with ½ teaspoon butter. Wrap securely in foil. Let rest for at least 15 minutes.
- Using a 2½-inch round cutter, cut 16 rounds from frozen sourdough-bread slices and 8 rounds from frozen wheat-bread slices. Cover with damp paper towels, or store in a resealable plastic bag to keep from drying out while preparing other ingredients. Let thaw completely (approximately 30 minutes).

- Using the same cutter, cut 8 rounds from cheese slices. Set aside.
- Fifteen minutes before serving, slice fillets into 4-x-¼-inch pieces. Set aside.
- Spread Horseradish Aïoli onto each bread round. Using 8 sourdough bread rounds (aïoli sides up) as bases, assemble sandwiches, stacking ingredients in the following order: 2 fillet slices (ruffled to fit bread rounds), cheese, a wheat bread round (aïoli side up), arugula, tomato slices, and a sourdough round (aïoli side down).
- Garnish each tea sandwich with a decorative pick, if desired.
- Serve immediately.

We used Penzeys Hungarian Style Half-Sharp Paprika, available at penzeys.com.

[†]*The best way to ensure meat reaches a safe internal temperature is to use a meat thermometer. Beef should be cooked to at least 140° (rare).*

Make-Ahead Tip: *Prepare beef tenderloin fillets no more than a day ahead. Wrap tightly in foil, and refrigerate until needed. Cut into slices 15 minutes before serving.*

Horseradish Aïoli

Gluten-free | Yield: ⅓ cup | Preparation: 5 minutes

⅓ cup mayonnaise
2 teaspoons prepared horseradish

- In a small bowl, combine mayonnaise and horseradish, whisking until smooth and creamy. Cover, and refrigerate until needed, up to 2 days.

"I shouldn't think even millionaires could eat anything nicer than new bread and real butter and honey for tea."

—Dodie Smith, *I Capture the Castle*

HAM AND CHIVE QUICHES
(recipe on page 51)

How-Tos

Let these step-by-step photos serve as your visual guide while you create these impressive and delicious teatime treats.

TARTLET CRUST

1

Using a cutter, cut shapes from dough.

2

Press dough shapes into tartlet pans.

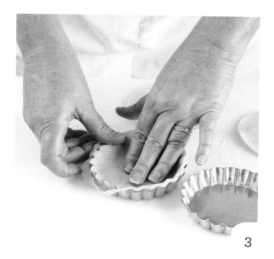

3

Trim excess dough.

4

Using the wide end of a chopstick, push dough into indentations of pan.

Arrange 3 bread rectangles, long sides together, alternating pumpernickel and rye. Spread a thick layer of herbed butter on top.

Place 3 more bread rectangles on top, alternating rye and pumpernickel.

Spread another layer of herbed butter on top. Finish with 3 more bread rectangles, alternating pumpernickel and rye.

Just before serving, using a serrated bread knife in a gentle sawing motion, cut sandwiches crossways into ½-inch slices.

SECTIONING AN ORANGE

| 1 | 2 | 3 |

Using a knife, trim both ends of an orange, creating a flat surface.

Turn orange on one end, and trim peel from sides.

Insert knife against the membranes dividing orange sections, and remove sections from orange.

MANGO CHUTNEY–CUCUMBER FLOWER CANAPÉS

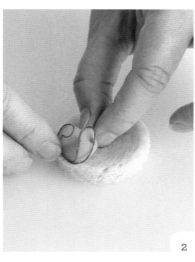

| 1 | 2 | 3 |

Fold very thin slices of cucumber in half, and fold again into quarters.

Place on prepared canapés with point facing the center.

Add four more folded cucumber slices, letting them unfold slightly to resemble the petals of a flower.

Acknowledgments

COVER
Wedgwood *Charnwood* teapot, cups and saucers, salad plate, and cream and sugar*. Maryland China Company *Bernadotte* gold-edged three-tier tidbit tray, 800-638-3880, *marylandchina.com*.

TITLE PAGE
Page 1: Wedgwood *Charnwood* teapot and five-piece place setting*. *Canterbury Classic* table topper†.

MASTHEAD
Pages 3–4: Royal Albert *Lady Carlyle* teapot, cups and saucers, and salad plates*. Maryland China Company *Bernadotte* gold-edged three-tier tidbit tray, 800-638-3880, *marylandchina.com*. *Canterbury Classic* table topper†.

TEA-STEEPING GUIDE
Page 9: *Blue Danube* teapot, cup and saucer, and salad plate*.

TEA-PAIRING GUIDE
Page 12: Wedgwood *Charnwood* teapot, cups and saucers, salad plate, cream, and sugar*. Maryland China Company *Bernadotte* gold-edged three-tier tidbit tray, 800-638-3880, *marylandchina.com*. *Canterbury Classic* table topper†.

SOUPS & SALADS
Pages 16–17: Raynaud *Allee Royale* dinner plate and salad plate, 732-751-0500, *devinecorp.net*. Pier1 gold charger, 800-245-4595, *pier1.com*. Juliska *Berry & Thread* glass bowl‡. **Page 18:** Royal Albert *Lady Carlyle* cream soup bowl*. **Page 19:** Royal Crown Derby *Titanic* five-piece place setting*. Gorham *Strasbourg* salad fork‡. **Page 20:** Royal Winton *Summertime* salad plate and square dinner plate; Hazel Atlas *Royal Lace* cream soup bowl*. **Page 22:** Herend *Fish Scale* dessert plate and cup and saucer, 800-643-7363, *herendusa.com*. **Page 23:** Villeroy & Boch *Wonderful World Orange* dinner plate*. Pier1 mini dessert bowls, 800-245-4595, *pier1.com*.
Page 25: Lenox Kate Spade New York *Bissell Cove* accent plate*. *Newport* table runner†. **Page 27:** Emile Henry rectangular platter, 302-326-4800, *emilehenry.com*. **Page 29:** Villeroy & Boch *Persia* cream soup bowl, 800-845-5376, *villeroy-boch.com*.
Page 30: Aynsley *Pembroke* crescent salad plate*. **Page 31:** Bernardaud *Artois Green* five-piece place setting*. *Vintage* silverplate five-piece place setting, 615-736-2892, *cakevintage.com*. **Page 32:** Maryland China Company *Bernadotte* gold-edged three-tier tidbit tray, 800-638-3880, *marylandchina.com*. **Page 33:** Wedgwood *Ascot* dinner plate and salad plate*. Juliska *Colette* dessert bowl‡. **Page 34:** Wedgwood *Charnwood* cups and saucers*. *Grantham* runner†. **Page 36:** Bernardaud *Eden Turquoise* salad plate and cup and saucer‡. **Page 37:** Royal Crown Derby *Aves Red* five-piece place setting*.

Page 39: Marchesa by Lenox *Spring Lark* five-piece place setting, 800-223-4311, *lenox.com*. World Market fluted silver chargers, 877-967-5362, *worldmarket.com*. Patricia Spratt *Whisper Paisley* tablecloth, 860-434-9291, *patriciasprattforthehome.com*. Juliska *Berry & Thread* glass bowl‡. **Page 40:** Wedgwood *Osborne* cream soup bowl, 877-720-3486, *wedgwoodusa.com*. **Page 41:** Bernardaud *Ecume White* dinner plate and salad plate, *bernardaud.fr*. **Page 42:** Royal Crown Derby *Aves Red* five-piece place setting and *Carlton Gold* salad plate*. Pier1 small glass, 800-245-4595, *pier1.com*.

QUICHES & TARTS
Page 45: *Blue Danube* salad plate and cup and saucer*. *Canterbury Classic* table topper†. **Page 48:** Royal Worcester *Regency Blue* dinner plate and salad plate*. **Page 49:** *Victorian Rose* doily†. **Page 51:** Vietri *Lastra White* handled rectangular platter, 919-245-4180, *vietri.com*. **Page 52:** White classic lace napkins, 800-243-0852, *surlatable.com*. **Page 53:** Lenox *French Perle White* hors d'oeuvres tray, 800-223-4311, *lenox.com*. **Page 54:** Maryland China Company *Bernadotte* gold-edged three-tier tidbit tray, 800-638-3880, *marylandchina.com*. **Page 56:** Wedgwood *Charnwood* square plate and cup and saucer*. *Canterbury* table topper†. **Page 57:** Spode *Fairy Dell* oval platter*. *Victorian Rose* doily†. **Page 58:** Herend *Chinese Bouquet Rust* dinner plate*. **Page 60:** Match 1995 Pewter two-tier stand, 201-792-5444, *match1995.com*. **Page 61:** Tag Furnishings ruffled-edge glass cake stand, 888-280-3321, *amazon.com*.
Page 63: Bernardaud *Ecume White* dinner plate, *bernardaud.fr*. **Page 64:** Royal Crown Derby *Derby Posies* teapot, 732-751-0500, *devinecorp.com*. *Canterbury Classic* table topper†. **Page 65:** Lenox *French Perle Ice Blue* four-piece place setting, 800-223-4311, *lenox.com*. **Page 66:** Comptoir de Famille Brasserie two-level serving tray, *comptoir-de-famille.com*. **Page 70:** *Shanghai* rectangular plate; aqua chambray crochet napkins, 877-967-5361, *worldmarket.com*. **Page 71:** Royal Albert *Lady Carlyle* platter*. **Page 72:** Pink cake stand**. **Page 73:** Wedgwood *Charnwood* salad plates*.

TEA SANDWICHES & CANAPÉS
Page 76: *Victorian Rose* doily†. **Page 77:** Pier1 lace edge plate and platter, 800-245-4595, *pier1.com*. **Page 78:** White scroll platter**. **Page 79:** Wedgwood *Ascot* salad plate and *Columbia Gold* dinner plate*. **Page 80:** Annie Glass ruffle tray‡. **Page 81:** Spode *Fairy Dell* oval platter*. **Page 84:** Vietri *Forma Cloud* rectangular platter, 919-245-4180, *vietri.com*. **Page 85:** *Canterbury Classic* table topper†. **Page 87:** Lenox Kate Spade New York *Wickford* oval platter, 800-223-4311, *lenox.com*. **Page 88:** Pier1 gold charger, 800-245-4595, *pier1.com*. Richard Ginori *Siena-Rust* teapot and cup and saucer*. Candlewick glass platter‡. **Page 89:** Bella Lux green platter**. **Page 90:** Cutwork platter**. **Page 92:** Wooden two-tiered stand,

800-243-0852, *surlatable.com*. **Page 93:** Emile Henry blue rectangular platter, 302-326-4800, *emilehenry.com*. **Page 96:** *Newport* doily/napkin†. **Page 97:** Annie Glass *Ruffle* platter‡. Raynaud *Allee Royale* teapot, 732-751-0500, *devinecorp.net*. **Page 99:** Villeroy & Boch *Wonderful World Green* service plate*. Crate & Barrel *Carson* picnic tablecloth, 800-967-6696, *crateandbarrel.com*. **Page 100:** Johnson Brothers *English Chippendale Red/Pink* five-piece place setting*. **Page 101:** Vietri *Incanto White Lace* small rectangular platter, 919-245-4180, *vietri.com*. Wedgwood *Sterling* cup and saucer and creamer, 877-720-3486, *wedgwoodusa.com*. **Page 104:** Whitewashed tiered stand, 888-779-5176, *potterybarn.com*. Wedgwood *Nantucket Basket* five-piece place setting, 877-720-34856, *wedgwoodusa.com*. **Page 105:** Juliska *Berry & Thread* medium rectangular gift tray; Herend *Fish Scale Green* cup and saucer‡. **Page 107:** Royal Albert *Lady Carlyle* tray‡. **Page 108:** Anna Weatherly sandwich tray†. **Page 109:** Ruffled-edge cake stand**. **Page 110:** Raynaud *Allee Royale* salad plate and dinner plate, 732-751-0500, *devinecorp.net*. **Page 112:** Wedgwood *Crown Sapphire* salad plate and cup and saucer*. **Page 113:** Royal Albert *Lady Carlyle* oval platter and cups and saucers*. *Canterbury Classic* table topper†. **Page 114:** Coalport *Ming Rose* platter*. *Canterbury Classic* table topper†. **Page 119:** Emile Henry white rectangular platter, 302-326-4800, *emilehenry.com*. **Page 120:** Coalport *Ming Rose* sandwich tray and cup and saucer*. **Page 121:** Castleton *Sunnyvale* platter*. *Canterbury Classic* table topper†. **Page 122:** White scroll platter**. **Page 125:** Wallace *Baroque* silverplate cake stand*. **Page 131:** Royal Albert *Lady Carlyle* teapot, creamer, sugar, cup and saucer, salad plate, and dinner plate*.

* *from Replacements, Ltd., 800-REPLACE,* replacements.com.
† *from Heritage Lace, 641-628-4949,* heritagelace.com.
‡ *from Bromberg's, 205-871-3276,* brombergs.com.
** *from HomeGoods, 800-888-0776,* homegoods.com.

Editor's Note: *Items not listed are from private collections. No pattern or manufacturer information is available.*

SPECIALTY TEA PURVEYORS
The teas recommended in the Tea-Pairing Guide on page 11 are available from one or more of these fine companies.

Capital Teas, 888-484-8327, *capitalteas.com*
Elmwood Inn Fine Teas, 800-765-2139, *elmwoodinn.com*
Global Tea Mart, 888-209-4223, *globalteamart.com*
Grace Tea Company, 978-635-9500, *gracetea.com*
Harney & Sons, 888-427-6398, *harney.com*
Simpson & Vail, 800-282-8327, *svtea.com*
Tealuxe, 888-832-5893, *tealuxe.com*
Teas Etc, 800-832-1126, *teasetc.com*

Recipe Index